# Dream Quest

## A Journey of Significant Vision

Including Inspirational Stories From Some
Amazing People I Met Along The Way

### Stephanie Wilson Halfacre

DQ
SPIRIT
WORKS

**Dream**Quest
A Journey of Significant Vision
*(Including Inspirational Stories From Some
Amazing People I Met Along The Way)*

**Published by**
DQ Spirit Works, LLC
Dayton, OH

# Dedication

This book is dedicated to God for enriching my life with many blessings and direction. Thank you for being that lighthouse and shining beacon in the storm and enabling me to live my dreams.

"I will instruct you and teach you in the way you should go;
I will counsel you with my loving eye on you."
*Psalm 32:8*
*New International Version (NIV)*

Mary was a true inspiration...

In memory of
**Mary Elizabeth Ford**
for her inspiring and entrepreneurial spirit
that she graciously shared with many.

## SPECIAL SECTION

# Foreword

Stephanie Halfacre is a rare combination of zeal and grace. In her first book she shares her "DreamQuest" and it really is a significant journey. There are other stories in the book that will encourage you on your "DreamQuest". Stephanie and her husband Stewart are dedicated Christians with a heart for people and a love for their church. It is my joy to serve as their pastor.

*Dr. Leon Stutzman, Bishop • Aspire Church*

Dream ON

"Go confidently in

the direction of your dreams.

Live the life you have imagined.

*—Henry David Thoreau*

# *Intro*duction
## Imagine your reality in dreams

As a young imaginative child, I was always fascinated by the beauty and grace of butterflies, especially the Monarch butterfly. There was nothing in the world I believed was more colorful than the vivid oranges and yellows of its silky wings. Occasionally on a warm summer day, I would run through my large hilly backyard and chase my favorite butterflies, hoping to catch one. I would patiently wait until a butterfly was gently resting on the pedal of a flower and carefully move toward its slowly flapping wings. Time after time, I would miss catching a butterfly by the sliver of a fingernail. It was almost as if the butterflies were playing a game with me. Even though I never was successful at my attempts, I just enjoyed their gentle graceful presence and sharing the backyard with them. One day, I prayed for God to let me catch my favorite butterfly. I learned at a very young age that God was good and listen to prayers — and I had faith and the innocence of a child that God would give me the desires of my little heart. During my prayer, I imagined and daydreamed of holding my hands out from my body and seeing a Monarch resting on my hands as though my fingers were flower pedals. It was only a short time before that wonderful image in my mind translated into reality. I caught a Monarch butterfly and it was the biggest one I had ever seen! This is one of my most magical childhood memories. It reminds me that God can help materialize your dreams if you have faith combined with a willingness for the seemingly impossible. Every time I see a butterfly now, I am transformed into a happy place — a place and time where dreams come true.

Why do adults lose that ability to dream — especially beyond their daily circumstances? When my twin daughters, Veronica and Victoria were 9 years-old, I would wonder where do they get all their imagination and energy to playfully create from dust. Veronica and Victoria would pretend to run their own restaurant (Red Joy) — of course, it was only a restaurant in the confides of our house. They would go to great detail to not only give us menus and receipts but actually prepare food! As adults, I believe we lose our insight because of circumstances or past failures. We use the past as barriers that block our future greatness that God has promised us. We miss so many opportunities when dreams are unfulfilled from lack of vision or action. Without any goals or awareness, dreams are just mental wanderings without direction and endless roads to nowhere. We can all find ourselves on the road to nowhere when the negative fallout of our daily routine radiates every inch of our souls.

Almost twenty-five years ago, I was suffering the results of an abusive relationship. There were many countless days when my whole body and soul was a deep dark void of emptiness. I was in a maze of confusion physically and spiritually. Every breath seemed to be controlled by my abuser. I asked the same question to myself every minute during that horrible time.

How do I escape a destructive environment that suffocates the fabric of my being? Anybody that has experienced any personal difficulty in life knows that there are no easy answers. It takes a personal metamorphic event — much like a butterfly whose life begins humbly, ending in magnificent beauty. Change if embraced will allow you to find beauty. Healing and growth involves a process of letting the problem go and acknowledging your worth as a person. God puts value in our worth and is bigger than any life difficulty that we encounter.

By sharing my personal experiences and the valued insights of my dearest friends, I hope that many readers will be inspired to overcome any obstacles that are blocking their path to abundant living. May you find the health and prosperous excellence that God has promised all of us. You can dream and live a journey of significant vision.

*Dreams realized can alter your reality*

METAMORPHIC

**"Yesterday is but today's memory,**

**tomorrow is today's dream."**

*— Kahlil Gibran*

# A *Dream* of Prophecy
## The Mysterious 8.8.8.8.10

What are dreams? Dreams represent a way of communication that thread our mind, body and spirit together. It is a combination of our conscious and subconscious mind trying to juggle seemingly random thoughts composed of daily events into some kind of logical order. Some dreams are like three-minute bouncy music videos, while other dreams may offer insight or resolution to a difficult problem. Scientist believe that human beings dream every night, although many people believe they hardly ever dream at all. Why do the majority of people forget their dreams? Is it because there is no conscious effort to remember or do we sometimes experience a memory block? Your dreams can float away as though they were light puffy clouds on a windy day.

During high school, I became committed to remembering every detail of my dreams. My dreams were so vivid and colorful; it was like watching television with my eyes closed. I even developed an ability to control my dreams. If there was a particular dream that was

> **"To accomplish great things, we must dream as well as act."**
> ▪ Anatole France

enjoyable, I would hope for a repeat performance. With very little effort, I could come back to the same place in the dream from the previous night. You have heard of TV on demand, well this is what I call dreams on demand. Unlike, most kids of my age, I looked forward to going to bed, because bedtime meant an entertaining night of endless dreams. I also discovered that dreams were not only a subconscious reflection of myself and relationship with others, but a spiritual connection to God as described by many events throughout the bible.

During a critical point in the relationship of Mary and Joseph, an angel of the Lord appeared in a dream; This is how the birth of Jesus Christ came about: His mother Mary was pledged to be married to Joseph, but before they came together, she was found to be with child through the Holy Spirit. Because Joseph her husband was a righteous man and did not want to expose her to public disgrace, he had in mind to divorce her quietly. But after he had considered this, an angel of the Lord appeared to him in a dream and said, "Joseph son of David, do not be afraid to take Mary home as your wife, because what is conceived in her is from the Holy Spirit. • Matthew 1:18-20 (NIV)

The Lord provided direction and guidance to Joseph in the essence of a dream. It was like a spiritual telegram. Joseph took action and fulfilled his position as Jesus' earthly father after hearing from God.

Some dreams can be described as watching a photo album being thrown in the air, while waiting to see where all the pieces are going to fall. The details are so random, it sometimes does not make any sense. Dreaming not only occurs while we are sleeping, but also during our conscious waking hours. Many times when my thoughts have drifted off to a virtual playground in my mind, it is almost like putting together a "to do" list, but without a pen or sticky pad. These are times when I entertain my goals and future desired accomplishments. I guess most people would call this daydreaming. It is an art that most school age children have mastered to perfection. Some adults, especially those that are raising young children believe daydreaming is a waste of time. I honestly believe daydreaming bridges the gap between dreams and reality. Dreams that occupy my attention and never leave my memory, are dreams that hold significant knowledge or vision.

Sometimes dreams provide an answer to an obstacle that we have been unable to hurdle. On a cold blustery morning in January 1986, I experienced an unusual dream that was so extraordinary that even after twenty-five years it is still touching every nerve ending of my soul today. As I slept on this typical winter day in Ohio, I began to dream and saw a row of houses. The houses, which were all the same in style, were very generic with hardly any detail or personality. Each house was the same close distance from each other and existed in a landscape void of people, trees, flowers, or grass. What could be significant about a repetitive row of generic houses that were similar to pieces on a Monopoly game board? At the time I lived with my husband and our baby daughter, Akiya (aka Tia) in Section 8 public housing. It was not the greatest place to live, but it was a modest home for our family. This at first glance could be a dream about where we currently lived and where we will possibly live in the future. Slowly the houses faded to darkness and I heard the loudest voice I have ever experienced while asleep or awake. The voice, which exhibited a powerful rich tone with a deep bass texture, was similar to the deepest soul shattering voice you would hear in a choir or R&B group. The image of the houses was only a movie trailer for the feature presentation. As the houses faded, a thunderous voice exclaimed 8.8.8.8.10!!! The sound was as loud as a thunderclap, but this was not a summer storm, it was a commanding voice of purpose. I immediately retreated from my dramatic vision and sat straight up against my pillow near the head of the bed. My total soul had been shaken. It was as though I was in a beehive that had just been bumped and all my internal thoughts were buzzing in unison. I knew in my heart, this was the voice of God. My excited spirit overflowed as I ran from the warm bed covers to tell my husband about my dream. He being a minister, interpreted my dream and proclaimed that we were going to be blessed with a new house. We were living in poverty in public housing, so who would not want this to be true? My spirit had been touched, and I knew that this message was much more than a blessing of a house. This was going to be the start of an altered state of existence.

My life during this time was not what I had expected. I grew up in my father's church and became an ordained minister at the age of fifteen. At a very young age I knew in my heart that God was the source of all the good things in life and that no problem was too big for his grace. In January 1986, I was in the third year of an abusive relationship. Before my amazing dream, I was searching for the strength and wisdom to keep my marriage together and happy. Divorce at that time did not qualify in my mind as an option. I had been taught that divorce was forbidden spiritually and culturally. Our family and many church members although aware of our constant difficulties, encouraged and expected us to stay together. I was very young and did not have the ability or courage at the time to consider anything beyond my circumstances. It was an existence of a limited perspective wrapped tightly in a daily routine. The 8.8.8.8.10 dream was a revelation from God and willingness for me to see beyond where I was and imagine the infinite places I could go. My long journey for a great change and opportunity had been birthed.

My dreams continued with a vivid voracity. Each night was filled with ripe anticipation. It was similar to experiencing tremors or aftershocks following a devastating earthquake. My foundation had been shaken and realignment was necessary. As each dream came to a refreshing conclusion, I noticed a couple of symbolic themes that presented a constant pattern of repetition. A majority of the dreams involved new houses. Unlike earlier, the houses were full of architectural detail and full of personality. I had never seen these homes before, but every square foot of each beautiful structure touched my soul with familiarity. There was one particular house that had large white pillars surrounding a large old-fashioned porch. Beyond the pillars, just through the front door sat a grand piano in a cozy living room trimmed in a natural wood. Many of the places were surrounded in happiness and the joyful presence

of my daughter and myself. My husband, who had become a destructive fixture in my life, was non-existent in any of my nighttime adventures. He could not see the vision because it was not intended for him. I believe all the images of beautiful homes were symbolic of provision and

**"For I know the thoughts that I think toward you, says the LORD, thoughts of peace and not of evil, to give you a future and a hope.."**
▪ Jeremiah 29:11 (NKJV)

not necessarily of material need. Our marriage would have not benefited from just moving our problems into a new house. We all resist change in our lives, even if change is obvious in a sea of horrible circumstances.

Although I had experienced an oppressive environment that sometimes deprived me of joy, I never forgot that God was my source of peace. Peace is a commodity that no human should be allowed to live without. Without a sense of comfort, we are all lost like tiny boats on a rough ocean. At nighttime God found me in a dream and let me know there was a new life of peace — a future with my little girl and without my oppressor. The 8.8.8.8.10 dream declared a new direction, although I did not fully understand the newly paved road erected up under my feet. It was similar to having your grade school teacher tell you about the importance of algebra when $c2 = a2 + b2$ seemed like complete alphabetical nonsense. Algebra did not make any sense to me because I did not have perspective to apply it to my everyday world. Through my dreams and desire for change I experienced a reborn perspective beyond present reality. Transformation would require plenty of time, action and faith in God. I was on a road to somewhere.

The road however, was not completely smooth and sometimes was littered with potholes. Through all the ragged detours, my life with my husband occasionally resembled a "normal" happy marriage. I experienced great joy in raising several foster children that needed loving attention — and at times I believed that he enjoyed the children also. I have discovered in my life that an unhappy person can not give happiness. There was a song in the late 1960s that said, "The love you take is equal to the love you make." I feel that he did not know how to reciprocate love and he was not a happy person.

During the fourth and fifth year of our marriage, my dreams continued to deliver symbolic images of escapism. One night during one of the turbulent times of our relationship, I dreamed I had entered a room with light, but no windows or doors. I then saw a room which seemed dark and I slowly tried to find my direction and senses. I realized entering into the room of darkness was a trap, so I stopped my forward progress abruptly, skidding across a slick floor. I sensed the enemy near me but I did not have time to stop and was consumed by the empty void. In the opposite direction of the dark room was a room of light. A voice echoed out of the light and said to remove the wall paneling. After removing the many pieces of wall paneling, I uncovered a strange closed door. My burning curiosity gave me the courage to open the mysterious door. I slowly pulled the door open and instantly found myself in a large maze that had many endless twist and turns. Another door appeared just as soon as I had stepped through the first entry way. Momentarily my eyes blinked a couple of times only to hear the same voice say, "You can choose to exit through the door or continue through a confusing maze." Without hesitation I chose to exit as quickly as possible. The second door was a passage way to a peaceful and calm space filled with soothing fresh air. I remembered taking a deep breath and exhaling so deeply, it was like I expelled all the painful hurt that I had experienced over the past few years. God let me know it was my decision to live in continuous confusion or a state of peaceful calm.

I struggled with ending my marriage even though it was not a healthy relationship. My grandparents had been married for 71 years at the time. I wanted to live "happily ever after" and had accepted for "better or for worse", but I knew deep down in my soul that better was never getting better and worse defined almost every aspect of our union.

Occasionally we all get wake-up calls that do not involve a buzzing alarm clock or someone nudging you. On February 7, 1988, I received a wake-up call that could possibly help me plan the rest of my life. It was our usual busy Sunday morning and I was getting my daughter and foster children ready for church. My husband, who needed no prompting or trigger, began one of his venomous tirades directed at me for no reason. The children had seen his angry behavior so many times, that as soon as we began to argue, they were conditioned to get dressed immediately. The arguments traditionally involved him verbally and physically abusing me and this was no different from any of the other awful fights. To my husband's surprise, this fight was very different because I chose to fight back as he choked me, wrenching my neck between his cold hands with unmerciful anger. Just like many times in the past, my husband stopped long enough from his grip on my neck to grab my house keys and say, "Get out of my house and walk to church!" My daughter and foster children, who were all barely dressed, left the house like it was on fire! As we stood on the concrete porch in the blustery cold, he decided to drive us to the church. I reluctantly, along with the children, got into the car. The children, frightened and cold, were as still as statues. The only noise audible in the car was the sound of the windows awkwardly rattling sporadically as the car rolled over bumps along the way. After the car came

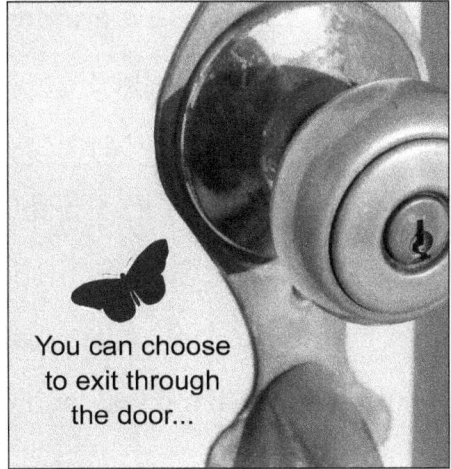

You can choose to exit through the door...

to, what seemed like a grinding stop at the church, I grabbed the children and walked up the church's steep steps as fast as humanly possible. My neck, which was bleeding was also pulsating with pain as a result of the early Sunday morning fight. Emotionally, I was tired, disgusted and humiliated, not only with the terrible past few hours, but the last four years of my life. My husband was an ordained minister and his horrible treatment of me is not what you would expect from a man of God. It is true that you can not judge a book by it's cover. From his outward appearances he was a "knight in shining armor", but his inner self was contaminated with anger and envy. He was a conflicted soul whose hidden contradictions occasionally rose to the surface like dirty sewer water. After entering the church, I collected my thoughts and walked to the office to call the police. The snooze button on my alarm clock was turned off and it is time to wake from this nightmare.

*Dreams open gateway to possibilities*

FLYING ABOVE THE STORM

> "Character is like a tree and reputation
>
> like a shadow. The shadow is what we
>
> think of it; the tree is the real thing.
>
> *— Abraham Lincoln*

# *On The* Road *Again*
## Finding My Own Path

The road had been long and sometimes plagued with uncertainty, but I knew God loved me. He had a plan for me that was rich with happiness and abundance — all I needed to do was take a chance and rely on his promise of mercy. After the Sunday morning fight in February, 1988, I finally found the courage to leave him. Although I knew it was the right thing to do, I still struggled with the guilt of failure. My fairy tale image of marriage had been corrupted and vandalized beyond recognition. I had made a commitment before God, family and friends that this marriage would survive through eternity. However, I finally realized that I had made a mistake but my mistake did not have to last forever. How do we get past the nagging guilt that sometimes lingers after realizing the consequences of a bad decision? I knew God loved me despite the mistakes. My being was not defined by the horrible relationship with him, but determined by my personal relationship with God. During my time away from my estranged husband, I was able to rest and pray for direction and peace daily.

After a few months of separation, even though my life and the life of my daughter were considerably better, I entertained thoughts of salvaging our marriage. Change is hard to embrace even though it is change for the good. During an early morning (about 2 a.m.) phone conversation in April, I told a close friend of mine that I was considering returning to my home. Was this the right thing to do or was it my reluctance towards ending a failed marriage? The truth was embedded in my subconscious mind but I needed to set it free — free from many entangled years of disillusionment and conflict. There is no problem bigger than God. Later that morning, I dreamed of a large ocean of blood. In this dream I was hemorrhaging to death. Usually when I dream, the difference between reality and fiction is obvious, but this vision was as real as every drop of red blood that flowed from my listless body. As my parents drove me to the hospital, I collapsed into the curvature of the car's cold back seat. My Mom and Dad told me they had tried to find my husband to inform him of my serious condition. In the dream I could see him, but he was far away in a blurred foggy distance supposedly hunting for a place for us to stay. My Dad was speeding toward the end of Nicholas Road where you had to make a left or a right turn. I heard the car come to an abrupt screeching stop. There was a brief sound of complete silence and then a voice from outside the car said, "You had a choice." I could feel my lifeless body, completely drained of blood, slowly fade away into nothingness. In my frightening dream I had died and left my daughter, Tia behind. Even though I was only experiencing a sub-conscious reality, my death and sense of abandonment felt horribly real. About 7 a.m. I immediately opened my heavy eyelids which seemed glued shut from the exhaustive adventure. 'You had a choice' repeatedly reverberated in my tired mind and body. I had died in my dream from a personal choice. It was a wrong choice with deadly consequences. Was this dream symbolic of a "spiritual" or "physical" death? A physical death would mean I leave Tia behind with her father who was not at the time capable of being a stable loving parent. The thought of a spiritual death horrified me, because that meant I had separated myself from God. If I had to choose, I would choose a physical death because I know deep in my heart that my soul is with God for eternity. God let me know that returning to the past was not the right decision for me or my daughter.

I collected the scattered thoughts bouncing in my head and told my mother about the dream. She had fearfully suspected that I was going back to my home and she prayed that I would not return to a destructive situation. My mother was relieved to know that I was finally comfortable with ending five years of a turbulent marriage. The cloud of

> **"But they that wait upon the LORD shall renew their strength; they shall mount up with wings as eagles; they shall run, and not be weary; and they shall walk, and not faint."**
> . Isaiah 40:31 (NKJV)

guilt and feeling of failure surrounding my relationship with him lifted like fog on a breezy summer morning. As though I was a captured butterfly, it was time to be set free from the net. My grandmother, Sadie, who was always a great role model in my life, gave me a crispy $100 dollar bill for a lawyer to get a divorce. At the time money was hard to come by and I really did not have enough for legal expenses. I prayed and asked God for a miracle. My estranged husband was still creating chaos although we were no longer together. He decided to forge my name on a joint tax return and he had received a tax refund that belonged to the both of us. The tax firm that prepared the taxes discovered his deception and immediately gave me a check for my rightful portion of approximately $170.00. I took this found money and my crispy $100 dollar bill that I had been holding onto and I gave my lawyer the $270.00 and asked him again if he would represent me. I knew that it was not enough to get a divorce. I needed money desperately, but mercy was more necessary than anything that a dollar could purchase. The lawyer shifted through the horrid details of the last five years and showed mercy and apathy toward my situation. My lawyer knew I needed to end my marriage immediately and was satisfied with the small amount of money that I offered him. Thank God for answering my prayer.

Ending my marriage was the right thing to do for myself and my daughter but the transition was very difficult. I gained peace but lost several things that were part of my life for the past five years. My daughter and I did not have a place of our own to stay, so I stayed with my parents. Not to mention, I also did not have a job or any health insurance. This was a new situation for me and a great struggle. I had always had a job and a place to stay. At the time my only alternative was to seek public assistance, but this was difficult to get because I was living with my parents and did not have my own home address. As strange as it sounds, to qualify for public housing assistance I needed some income and a place of my own (other than my parent's house). I was also accustomed to going to the doctor and now the doctor's office did not want to see us because there was no health insurance. Without a penny in your pocket, choices are limited. If I wanted medical care, I had to go to the "free" clinic. Nothing in life is "free". They also required some type of monetary payment. How do you pay when you have no income? What was God's plan for us? I knew God was still there but I was battling with the pressure of daily survival. I was so wrapped up in my difficulties that depression began to take a toll on my body. My faith and trust in God kept me from rolling off a jagged cliff at 100 mph. I constantly told myself that this situation was only temporary and my life would improve dramatically. I must begin again.

My dramatic unusual dream of the 8.8.8.8.10 which I had almost forgotten was in the distant past and I was still unaware of the significance in relationship to my life. I was finally free from my marriage and the maddening world that we existed in. I was staying with my parents but needed a place of my own where my daughter and I could live peacefully. When you are a single parent (especially a woman) and do not have any means or money, your choices are limited regarding a decent place to stay. After several failed attempts to get public assistance, I had become exhausted. This routine had become frustrating and I felt like I was running in circles. As I stood at the bus stop, after one of those failed attempts at the welfare office, I decided that I was not going back to my parent's home without my own income. It was the end of the day and I was drained. I needed resolution, so I prayed and asked God for his mercy. The walk from the bus stop back to the welfare office seemed shorter as I gained confidence with every step. The same caseworker, who I wanted to kill just moments before, decided to help me and mercy had prevailed again! She gave me a check, (yes, money!), and told me to use the check as proof of income to get qualified for housing. This was my first (and most difficult) experience with the Welfare system.

I finally qualified to get a place of my own in a local public housing complex. Although the welfare system helps a lot of people, the process was riddled with lots of trap doors, especially for someone dealing with it for the first time. The public housing agency gave you three choices of apartments to live. The first two choices were located in areas of the complex that appeared to be unsafe and infested with drug activity. I needed a place to stay that was safe for my daughter and me. They could not understand why I refused the first two locations. I desperately needed a place to stay, but that place had to offer security. Once again God showed me his endless mercy. My third and final choice was an apartment located in the front area of the complex. It was located on a noisy and busy street, but it was away from the drug dealers that openly did business in the back. I was also concerned about my ex-husband finding me. The divorce settlement gave him visitation privileges, but I always arranged for our daughter to be picked up at my parent's house to protect my security and privacy. At the time I was placed in the apartment I did not realize that this location was the most desirable place to be in the complex. It was not what I envisioned years ago when I had the numerous dreams about the nice houses but I was starting from scratch and beggars can not be choosers. I prayed and asked God for his protection. Psalms 91 describes a secret place and how God will hide us. It also speaks of deliverance and preservation. During the early hours of my first night in my apartment I was startled out of a deep sleep by several loud and unfamiliar clicking sounds. I immediately realized that the strange sounds were gun shots outside my bedroom window. It was very clear to me that my new home was just a temporary place to stay. It was very uncomfortable and awkward for me. I was like a gold fish in a bird's nest.

In the late 1980s, my father preached a sermon in church that echoed in my spirit. He said, "If you do not like where you are in life, change what you are doing". I definitely did not want to stay where I was. Out and up were the two directions I needed to go. It was my desire to eventually get out of public housing and move upward towards an abundant life God had promised in Malachi 3:10. I was so financially shackled in my situation that pennies in the dark hidden pockets of my purse squeaked from the daily stretching.

There is beauty and truth in the smallest gestures of favor we receive. When you are hungry, that first tiny bite always seems the most pleasurable. I had so many needs in my life during the late 1980s including the desperate need for a good pair of shoes. My shoes were so worn and hole ridden that I entertained going barefoot. Every step was an adventure and just walking across the street was dangerous because the shoes were very slippery. I did not have any money, but I did possess a department store credit card. Unfortunately, the credit card was just a piece of useless plastic, because the balance was at the allowed maximum limit. At this point, the fear of having my card declined at the checkout line was not my main concern. I needed a new pair of shoes. So, I made up my mind and went to the store to shop. As I gazed at the hundred of colorful fashion choices, my only goal was to find the most least expensive shoe on the sales rack. I found a plain pair of shoes that were not especially fancy or trendy in style.

However the price was attractive for less than twenty dollars not including the sales discount. During my walk toward the cashier, I prayed that I would be able to get those shoes. I slowly put the shoes and my credit card on the glass counter next to the cash register. The pleasant cashier scanned the shoe box. After the sales discount, the shoes were only ten dollars. If the shoes were any cheaper, they would have been free but unfortunately my finances made free not affordable. As my credit card was swiped, I stood quietly and hoped for my credit to be approved. It seemed like an eternity. The cashier finally looked away from the cash register and she said, "I am sorry, but your card has been declined." Having your credit declined is an embarrassing moment for anyone, but I was more embarrassed by my broken down shoes. Before my heart could sink, I showed the cashier my horribly worn-out shoes. She briefly and patiently looked at my feet through the many holes in the fabric and then called her manager. Mercy prevailed and the manager approved my purchase. It is a great example of how small gestures can lift you beyond your negative circumstances. My new shoes did not stay in the box very long as I immediately threw out my rags and literally skipped out of the store like a fashion model strutting down a runway strip to the bus stop. This signaled a step in the right direction. The scripture Psalms 23 states, "Surely goodness and mercy shall follow me all the days of my life."

I was very grateful to God for his grace. As I prayed and continued to seek God's guidance, I realized that I had a gift from the past that was not being used. During my marriage my ex-husband and I enjoyed foster parenting many children. Even though my marriage was rocky, I always experienced unmeasurable joy and love from the boys and girls I cared for. It was a two-way street that joined in the middle. The

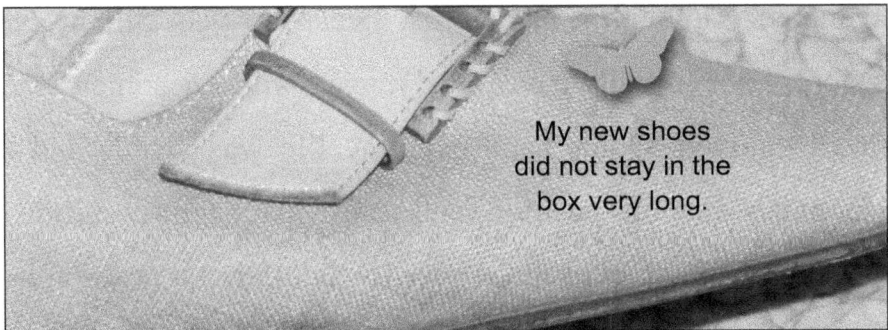

My new shoes did not stay in the box very long.

children received lots of love and returned genuine affection instinctively. My daughter was also happy to have brothers and sisters to play with.

I did not have a job, which gave me the opportunity to volunteer in the children's school on a daily basis. It was rewarding to participate with my children, as well as other students. I was at school so often that many of the parents and students thought I was a teacher. The children's boundless energy and hyperactive imagination was always very contagious and soothing to my spirit. I knew that I was making a dramatic positive difference in the lives of my foster children and all the students at school. At the end of the school year, one of the teachers asked me to consider applying for one of the clerical positions that was available. Although it made sense because I was a fixture at school, I never really envisioned myself working somewhere that I enjoyed. God's hand over my life was visible and I recognized that this position was custom made for my abilities and talents. The next school year I was offered a position as a paraprofessional in the childcare department instead of the clerical position that I was qualified for. Although it was only a part-time substitute position, I was eventually working full time hours. It was strange because I had an associate degree in business administration, but I was happily working in the school's daycare. It is all about timing. You can not catch a bus before it gets to the bus stop and you can not get on a bus without a destination. God knew where I was going and what time I would get there. With great patience, I believed that eventually the clerical position would be offered to me. I was in the perfect place to get a position. I took nothing for granted and enjoyed working in the childcare department. During my breaks, I would routinely walk down the hallway to the computer lab to practice my typing. I graduated from college a couple of years before the desktop computer age and had only used word processors (typewriters). What is a mouse? I was only familiar with the four-legged creatures that made me scream at the top of my lungs. Technology and I were as compatible as dogs and cats in a very small room without an exit. I was very unfamiliar with the new technology but this was preparation for the future. The possibilities were great with nothing to loose. I was so motivated to succeed that I would have picked-up a real mouse if it were attached to a computer. Without computer skills there was absolutely no way I would be able to accomplish my goal of getting a clerical position. I was like a squirrel gathering nuts in the winter — it was about doing what was necessary and preparation. God was leading the way. All I had to do was to follow the paved path and be diligent in all my efforts toward self improvement. It was my choice to work hard to achieve my dreams. I just had to do the hard work. God promised us abundant life. Why eat a plain hamburger, when you can enjoy a juicy mouth watering steak? I wanted the best in life that was possible. Not only did I want success for myself but for everyone I knew. Sometimes, we do not realize the power we possess as individuals and the positive effect we have on others in our proximity. We are here to help one another, if only by example, but we must help ourselves first.

THE JOY OF HARMONY

"He is richest who is content

with the least, for content

is the wealth of nature."

— *Socrates*

# *Relationship of* PEACE
## The process of contentment

I have always been fascinated by the unique beauty of the lighthouse. Lighthouses served the purpose of guiding ships at sea to their final destination. Their bright oscillating beacons light a path through total darkness, thick opaque fog or vicious storms. Through my life, and especially the past couple of years, God has truly been my beacon of security. I literally would have been lost out at sea and ship wrecked along the jagged rocks without his guidance. My close relationship with God has made me a better person. I want to share the better person with my family, friends, co-workers and everyone I meet.

I was a minister in my father's church and occasionally I was given the opportunity to preach. In late December 1989, I delivered a message about the "Walls of Jericho Coming Down". As I accepted the abundance and blessings of God, I rejected the spirit of poverty. Why live a life of discouragement when God has promised all of us a great supply of the best. With great impulsive excitement, during the message, I proclaimed I was going to get a "new car", maybe a 1987 or 1989. The pastor immediately responded and suggested, why not get a "brand new 1990 car"? Why do we always put limits on God and in the process limit ourselves from experiencing every great opportunity? I know we are told everyday by someone that we can not have something. If we listen, we can condition ourselves to expect less in every situation. With God, we have a giant ocean of possibilities which go beyond probability when we make an effort to reel in our catch. Although I had never considered owning a new car, not to mention parking a brand new car in the front section of the housing projects, I began to visually see myself behind the wheel of a shiny brand new car. The vision was so real I could see my daughter and her foster sisters, all openly grinning, buckled-up on the soft vinyl back seat. A search began, which would have been unimaginable a year ago, for my car. Just the thought and privilege of looking for a new car was overwhelmingly exciting. Every time I went to visit a car dealership, my heart would jump with ripe anticipation. It was fun just looking! In February of 1990, I purchased a brand new 1990 Chevy. It was a pretty sky blue color with only ten miles on the odometer. I was grateful to God for the wonderful blessing.

Now that I had a new car, it was time to get a new home. Parking a car, especially a brand new car, in the housing projects was very risky because vandalism and auto theft was a

> **"Imagination is everything. It is the preview of life's coming attractions."**
> ▪ Albert Einstein

part of the daily events where I lived. I did not take things for granted. After riding the bus everywhere, I knew it was a privilege to have any form of transportation. I had to take care of my investment. Even good changes can present challenges that need to be addressed. This was part of a big picture of improvements in my life. I just needed to make the adjustment to make forward steps. I really did not need a reason to move from the housing projects, but the car created a good excuse. This was not a permanent home for me. Mentally, I had my bags packed the first day I moved in, so this was a welcoming change. I knew my next residence would be an improvement compared to where I was. Through a friend at church I was able to rent a house on Salem Avenue. It was a warm and beautiful larger older home with huge rooms in a residential area. This really felt like a real home, nothing like my former housing, which was only a temporary place to stay. Although, once again I was on a very busy main street, God hid my whereabouts from my ex-husband. Later, I eventually moved into a house on Cicillion Avenue, a quiet dead end street. It was the first time I had been on a quiet street since the divorce and it was very calm and peaceful. My life was significantly different than from a few years ago because not only have I found direction, but I have been given peace. God is good.

At a young age my father taught me the power of tithing. I

have always been a consistent tither. Tithing is the practice of giving the first 10 percent of everything you receive or earn. God promises that if you give, you will receive a blessing that is unmeasurable. I began to ask myself if you trust the Lord, why stop at 10 percent. So, I have made an effort to give more than 10 percent. The proof is in the pudding (or blessings). When I was with my ex-husband, it was difficult to tithe because, although he was a minister, he did not want me to give my tithes. He was the Scrooge of giving. Although he objected, I continued to tithe as much as possible against a tide of constant resistance. I began to tithe with a full heart and freedom after the divorce. As God always honors his promises, my disappointment was replaced with continuous blessings and opportunities. At the end of each year after my divorce, the accountants at church were always amazed that I was one of the biggest tithers, although I was a single mother on a modest income. I simply understood the principles of sowing and my connection with God. If a farmer purposes himself to yield a bigger crop then the previous year, he must first plant more seeds and then believe in the process. This will result in a larger harvest. Just call me Mrs. Johnny Appleseed because I am sowing and planting across the land so my harvest will be plentiful.

When you find God, I believe you find yourself. During my marriage, I spent a large part of my day being under the rule of my husband. He dictated my life, my life at church and my life outside the home. He was a dictator with an iron hand and unfortunately I was the subject of his control. The daily controlling treatment sucked the air from my lungs and personality from my soul. I could never be myself when I was married to him. Although I had been divorced for several years, I still carried personal scars that hid my inner beauty behind a shell of insecurity. I asked God to give me freedom to let me be me and allow my inner self to shine with a crystal clear clarity. I wanted to be physically, emotionally and spiritually strong for myself so that I could benefit my family as well as my neighbors. Without clarity, you can not even help yourself.

As I relaxed, I felt the shell slowly fade away and I felt more comfortable in my inner skin. Now it was time to change how I covered and decorated my outer skin.

Growing up in a Pentecostal church meant dress apparel, especially for women, was very conservative. Long dresses down to the ankles and blouses that buttoned-up right below the chin were standard uniforms. The only skin that was visible was your hands and face. Facial make-up of any kind was also considered a tool of the devil. It was a very rigid dress code, culturally dictated in the church, specifically designed to control women. As I matured, I did not understand why I had to dress like a girl growing up on a 19th century farm. We were not riding around in horse-drawn wagons on unpaved dusty trails. Some churches eventually discovered that saving souls had nothing to do with the type of clothes on your back. It was about creating positive change in people's hearts and building a personal relationship with God. I desperately wanted out of my "fashion" prison. As the warm summer air slowly rose with each sunrise, so did the hemline of my skirt. My very long old fashioned skirts started to spend less time on me and more time in the corner of a dark closet on a hanger. I bravely purchased a couple of opened neck vividly tinted shirts to compliment my new feminine skirts. After more than twenty-five years buried in conservative church culture, I was practically a rebel. For some people that knew me, the change in my appearance probably seemed very sudden and drastic. During a business conference, I wore a pretty blue and white dress that was almost one inch above the knees. It was almost two feet shorter than any other dress, (except for the new skirts), that currently existed in my puritan wardrobe. I arrived at the conference a little apprehensive about the possible reactions to my new wardrobe — not that I really expected any comments or even compliments. My mom who has always been able to express herself was unusually silent. By the startled expression I was certain she was in some type of shock. My father who was a man of few (very few) words, actually liked my dress and told me so. I knew I had arrived when I managed to leave my mother speechless and make my father speak. My new clothes were an expression of the peace and freedom I had found. I was ready to leave my past behind just like the old dusty clothes that were hung in the back of the closet. I had always

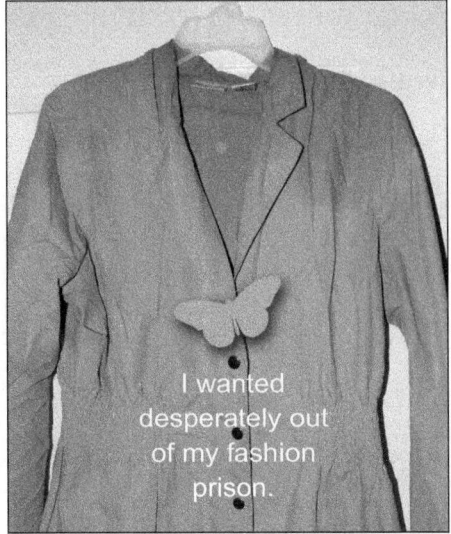

I wanted desperately out of my fashion prison.

wanted to dress differently but did not have enough courage. The new me is just the old me uncovered.

Over the past few years I have grown accustom to a world of change, so no circumstance or new situation surprised me. Maybe I just learned from past experience that it is better to go with the flow then to fight with the tide. As the end of the school year approached, the school board made a financial decision to layoff employees with less than three years of service. Unfortunately I had only been employed in the daycare center for two years. In the past, this kind of unexpected news would have completely thrown me off balance. It was going to be a disruption of my daily life and I really would miss my relationships that I had developed with the children and their parents. Even good things sometimes come to an end so that there can be a starting point for a better experience. I chose to remain positive because I knew that God was in control and there was no reason to panic. From my perspective, there was a bright side to this seemingly bad news. The winter season and I do not agree. Frigid temperatures, ice, and snow should only be for the penguins. My nature is more compatible with soft sandy beaches that glide along a crystal blue ocean but unless you happen to be glancing through a travel brochure, this is just an exotic daydream in the four seasoned climate of Ohio. So the layoff was not so bad. When the coldest months of the year arrived, I would not have to fight the harsh elements traveling to work in the dark early morning hours. It was a blessing to have the privilege of taking a break and I knew this was only a temporary vacation away from working. I planned to enjoy my "free" time while it lasted.

The summer season was simmering down and my unusual summer vacation is now permanently extended due to the layoff. Although financially I had been affected, I had no problems taking care of a household which included my daughter and two foster daughters (Dawana and Shelly). The mailbox was a window of supernatural blessings. Occasionally, I would open my mailbox and find anonymous letters that read, "The enclosed check is for your utilities this month". Sometimes the letters would come directly from the creditors with big red letters stamped in the upper right-hand corner that read "Paid in Full". Creditors do not usually make the habit of writing off a responsibility of debt. God is good! In late September, my younger sister, (Karen) and I took advantage of a special discount and purchased round trip airline tickets to Europe for less than $500.00 a piece. The trip to Germany was to see our brother (Mark) and his family and it was scheduled for March of the following year. I knew possibly that I could be working before March and this could interfere with the trip overseas. It was an opportunity of a lifetime to travel outside the country for less than the usual price.

Life sometimes can offer surprising twists but we just have to be ready to navigate the curvy winding roads that are just ahead of us. A couple of months later, (in November 1992), I received one of those surprising twist in the form of a telephone call. The City of Dayton government office, called to offer me a clerical position that was currently available. During my employment at the Dayton Board of Education, (on the advice of my co-workers), I would occasionally take civil service tests for a promotional opportunity. Those days of sneaking off to the computer lab during my work breaks to improve my skills, seemed like a distant lifetime ago. I hadn't forgotten about my desire to get a job that complimented my college training. It wasn't about if, but when my clerical job would materialize. A watched pot never boils and a great opportunity is never available until you are ready. With great excitement and anticipation I graciously accepted the job offer which was a great position with great benefits. Now I had a dilemma. Would I be able to travel to Europe in March and be away from a new job for three long weeks? My two opportunities had collided like two bumper cars cruising head-on at an amusement park. It was fun and unsettling at the same time. As an added complication, all new hires were given six months probation which translated into absolutely no vacation time for the first 180 days on the job. The math in my head concluded that my first chance at a vacation would be in May. This was almost two months after the European trip I had already paid for was suppose to take place. It was a real dilemma. I prayed that my new employers would understand and give me a thirty day break from the usual probation period. Miraculously during the hiring process, I explained my situation and they agreed to delay my probation

> **"But my God shall supply all your need according to his riches in glory by Christ Jesus.."**
> ▪ Philippians 4:19 (NKJV)

obligation during my trip. After working a couple weeks, my co-workers were very surprised (shocked) that management had given me permission to delay the lengthy probation period for a vacation. Even if I had worked a year without a break, I still would have not accumulated even two weeks of paid vacation. This was a miracle. I was able to have my cake and eat it too. I was very grateful for my new job and the plane tickets.

Life sometimes resembles a box of Cracker Jacks with a yummy caramel coated popcorn hiding a special individually wrapped surprise. It was December of 1992, I had only worked a few weeks in my new position, when I was approached by a strange man. Charles Dannin, who I barely knew, was one of my co-workers. He introduced himself and then awkwardly asked me a very personal question. Are you single, married, or available? The question, especially from someone I had just met, caught me by surprise so quickly and made every drop of blood rush from my head. For a brief second, I was at a loss for words. Was he asking for himself or someone else? Before I could respond, Charles immediately explained that his wife (Rosemary) worked with a man who desperately needed to get a "real life" and if I would be interested in meeting him. The description of Charles wife's friend did not instantly impress my curiosity. At the time, I was dating occasionally, but a "knight in shining armor" was not what I needed. This man, who needed to get a life, did not resemble my fairy tale prince. Against most of the reasonable voices in my mind, I agreed to meet the mystery man.

*Peace breeds productivity and creativity*

SPREADING MY WINGS

"Loyalty to a petrified

opinion never yet broke a chain

or freed a human soul."

— *Mark Twain*

# *When I Met STU*
## Uncovering the "mystery man"

A new year has always been exciting to me because it brings expectations and possibilities. It is life's do over. January 1st is like having a clean and shiny blank blackboard and several boxes of white dusty chalk in front of us. We just need to take the chalk, get our hands dirty and write something. I had resolved in my heart to make the next 365 days of my the life the best I have ever lived. It is a good feeling when you can say yesterday was good, but today is going to be much better. God has promised us a world of abundance and I am ready to receive the best.

It is five years after my divorce and I no longer have those haunting dreams of a vicious black dog with razor sharp teeth trying to bite me repeatedly. The terrifying dream was symbolic of my nightmare marriage, which is in the distant blurry past. I only talk to my ex-husband during his occasional visitation appointments with our daughter. The scary "dog attack" dreams have changed and are reflective of my new independent confidence. Now when I dream, the black dog that once chased me down is restrained by a very short chain with a tight noose-like collar that has rendered that crazy canine harmless. Even the dog's ferocious bark, which generated deep terror in my soul, now sounds like the whimper of a tiny puppy. I am safe and out of reach.

The year 1993 began with an atmosphere of contentment because not only did I have a new job and a peaceful quiet home, but I was also looking forward to my European vacation in March. My life was wonderful and I did not need or want anything. I was happy and thankful! On a cold winter day, Sunday, January 3, 1993, after returning home from church I received a phone call from the "mystery man", the friend of my co-worker's wife who desperately needed to "get a life". My intention was to meet the "mystery man" with no expectations. I was not looking to date anyone or put energy into a relationship. The phone call was very brief and did not reveal much about the "mystery man" except that his first name was Stewart. After a short introduction of ourselves, we decided that the following Sunday would be our first date — a real "blind date". I had no thoughts of what to expect but I was neither excited or nervous about meeting Stewart. My attitude was neutral.

On Saturday, January 9th I called Stewart to cancel our first meeting. The weekend had not gone well for me and I was not in my normal pleasant mood. A "blind date" at the moment was not at the top of my priority list. Although my expectations were

> **"When one door of happiness closes, another opens, but often we look so long at the closed door that we do not see the one that has been opened for us."**
> ▪ Helen Keller

low, I wanted our first meeting to be without distractions. Maybe subconsciously I wanted Stewart to be discouraged, because I was not sure if he would still be interested. Once again our conversation was short and we agreed to delay our date until the following Sunday.

During the next week I occasionally thought about my upcoming date with Stewart, the "mystery man". The thoughts were brief daydreams that evaporated like steam as soon as they crept into my head because the routine of every day life was more important to me than meeting a stranger. After a long work week, Sunday, January 17th finally arrived and it was no different than any other Sunday in the middle of winter. It was a cold blustery day and all I wanted to do was stay inside where it was warm and not venture outside in the frigid temperatures to meet someone that I did not know. Even though I would have rather jumped under a blanket, I decided to keep my commitment and meet Stewart.

Earlier during the week, my mother had agreed to babysit the girls while I was on my date. Sometime plans, even the best plans, can change like the weather in Ohio. The plan was to drop the girls off at my parent's house, but my Mom at the last minute decided that she could not babysit. My parents had become concerned about the "mystery man" and whether it was safe for me to go on a blind date. I did not want to call Stewart and cancel our date again. It was frustrating because I was a grown woman, but my parents were making decisions for me like I was a little lost school girl. Maybe they had visions of me being kidnapped and tied-up in some dark damp basement in an unknown location. This was not my first blind date and I was perfectly comfortable with meeting someone I did not know. At the last moment, my youngest brother Steve decided to watch the girls. This was a small miracle, because Steve had never baby sat for me before. The clock was ticking so loud it was blaring and I needed to get home and get ready for my date.

On the drive home from my parents house I was still gathering my thoughts about meeting someone "new". I was at a point in my life where I was not looking for a husband, not even a boyfriend. During my first marriage I was very naive and can remember "looking for" and asking God for a husband. This resulted in a bad marriage because I was not specific in what I wanted in a loving

> **"He who finds a wife finds a good thing, And obtains favor from the LORD."**
> ▪ Proverbs 18:22 (NKJV)

relationship. At the time I did not adhere to what the bible says about marriage: "He who finds a wife finds a good thing." Now I realize if there is someone (a true soul mate) meant for me, they would have to find me. Although I was not in a hurry, I still prayed that God would some day give me a husband that is wonderful beyond my imagination.

As I arrived at my house, I decided to treat my blind date like a job interview and I wanted my first impression to be good. I was at a place of peace with myself and God. Although I am still not expecting much, I wanted Stewart to see that I was someone special. Inside my closet, I found a nice suit to wear along with matching shoes. I combed my hair until every stray hair was in place. My make-up complimented my clothing and hair in near flawless perfection. I was ready for my "interview/blind date".

I could hear a car in my driveway and soon there was the sound of a door closing. As I began walking to the front door, a series of soft knocks could be heard. I opened the door and a tall African-American man introduced himself as Stewart. He was neatly dressed in a blue jacket, sweater, dark slacks and nice shoes. As we walked to his car, Stewart was a gentleman and opened the passenger door for me. Along the 15 minute ride to a local restaurant, there were exchanges of pleasant small talk. At the restaurant, we were seated by the waitress at a window that faced the west and slowly setting sun. Even though it was very cold, it was a "good" winter day with bright sunshine peaking through some pretty white puffy clouds.

The food and conversation were both plentiful and good. It was easy talking to Stewart because he was down to earth. He genuinely wanted to know about me and did not mind sharing details about himself. During somewhere in the conversation,

Stewart became very relaxed and told me that he had holes in the bottom of his shoes and that his feet got wet when it rained. What? Was this a test to make me run to the door and end the date, which to this point had been very good? I actually did not think much about it, because I remember a time in my life when there were holes in my shoes. The "blind date" had actually materialized into a nice evening shared by two people who found a lot in common.

On the way home, we talked more than on the way to the restaurant and we seemed to have more to talk about. Even though our meeting was nice, (especially for a first date), I had no intentions of seeing him again. My life was very comfortable and ridiculously routine — you could almost describe it as boring. It was like watching clothes dry on a clothes line. I had everything I needed and the only thing I lacked was chaos. A lack of chaos was a good thing for me and my girls. Stewart was a nice looking well-mannered man with a good personality and we discovered that we shared a lot in common, but I was not looking for anyone. During our conversation, he may have mentioned he wanted to get married someday in the near future but my ears pretended not to hear him. Once again I thought, I am not looking for a husband. One thing about Stewart that remained constant throughout the evening was his good manners. It is hard to find a thoughtful individual who actually cares about others and not the selfish inward needs of themselves. He was a genuine gentleman. As we arrived at my house, Stewart walked me to the door, gave me a warm handshake, and then quietly drove away.

The sun setting into the cold winter sky marked an end to a good evening. During the drive to my parents house to pick-up my girls, I reviewed my date with Stewart in my mind several times. My parents, who had tried to discourage me from going on my blind date, were filled with curiosity and asked me immediately about my evening. I think they expected me to say, "You were right , Stewart was a creepy crawly monster and I wish I had not meant him today!" When I told my father and mother that Stewart was a nice gentlemen, I could not tell if they were surprised or disappointed. My father was still concerned and believed it was still too dangerous to go on a blind date. In my daily life I always took precautions and let my family know where I was going, besides I knew God was watching over me. My parents concern was just useless worry, because I had no plans to go on any dates or blind dates in the near future.

The weekend was over and on Monday I returned to work and like every other Monday before that, I was back to my routine. I thanked Charles for having introduced Stewart to me and let him know that I had a wonderful evening. Charles asked if I had plans on seeing Stewart again, to which I replied, no.

About the middle of the week I found a surprise in my mailbox among the other usual bills and junk mail. Stewart had sent me a thoughtful "homemade" card thanking me for our recent date and his desire to see me again. He really wanted to see me again? The following day, he called and asked me to go out on another date and of course, I was still not interested, and told him I was not available. Prior to our first date, I had grown tired of the dating game. I did not have the desire to devote time to meaningless relationships that brought negative energy to my happy life. Although he was always polite, Stewart was very persistent, (like a solicitor), and called again a couple days later. It seemed like he was going to keep calling until I agreed to see him again. This time, I was sick, so I had a good excuse to say no but I was not sure if Stewart believed me. If I were him, I would have probably never called again. I would have taken the hint after the 2nd or 3rd time and just disappeared forever. If I did not know any better, I was starting to think that Stewart was on a mission. Call it "mission Stephanie". Like a consistently ticking clock, Stewart once again called me this time to see how I was feeling but I was still sick. He immediately, without skipping a beat, said, "I can bring something over to your house to make you feel better as well as some brownies for the girls." The word no had become a familiar word in my vocabulary, but now I had to say yes this time. After about 90 minutes had passed, there was a soft knock at my door, like there was the first time we met. I opened the door and it was Stewart holding a vase of flowers. The vase was an old 16 oz. Pepsi bottle that was spray painted white. It was unique and pretty. He also brought with him a pan of brownies that were still warm. And that was not all, for my health, Stewart gave me an orange with a decorative gift bow attached. If he was trying to impress me, he did! I invited Stewart to stay and eat some brownies while we watched television. His kindness and caring spirit captured my heart and melted my relenting reluctance. I was ready for his friendship.

Over the next couple of weeks the person I once referred to as the "mystery man" had become a good friend. We enjoyed seeing each other and talking occasionally over the phone. We were building a good foundation in our relationship. When February 14th, Valentines Day, arrived, I did not know what to expect from Stewart. We were friends but this was a romantic holiday. I knew Stewart had a romantic spirit and would not miss giving me something to commemorate the "day of love", so I was a little nervous. He did not disappoint me and arrived at my door with a big gift bag. I reached deep in the gift bag to find a calendar book and a gift card. It was a from a clothing store. More specifically, it was a lingerie store I had never visited before. In only a few weeks I have discovered that Stewart is creative and likes to do things a little different. Along with each gift, there were special instructions for me to follow. For the beautiful calendar, I was instructed to write down anything special about our relationship over the next year. The calendar had plenty of lines and spaces to write, kind of like a diary. The gift card had a higher degree of difficulty. Stewart told me I had to buy something from the lingerie store

His kindness and caring spirit captured my heart.

and model whatever I purchased. At first I was not sure what to think, especially since I had never been to this particular store before. I was raised in the old fashioned church. My roots were conservative down to my underwear. This was exciting and scary at the same time because Christian women, I thought, did not shop in these kinds of places. Then I thought to myself, it is just clothing.

A few days later I went to the "clothing" store. Once inside, I realized that there were many things to buy besides lingerie. Not only was there underwear, but perfumes, lotions and clothing (the outside kind of clothing). It was a refreshing new experience for me. I took my time and carefully picked out an item that I could purchase with my gift card, knowing that I had promised to model whatever I bought for Stewart to see. After a few days I had Stewart come over to my house and ask him to have a seat on the sofa so I could model the gift I had especially selected. He had no idea what I had bought and I was not sure what he expected. We were both like little children anticipating some big magical event. As he sat patiently on the edge of the sofa, I walked into the next room and paused for several minutes (I did this to build the excitement). Just before I returned to the room where Stewart sat patiently waiting, I asked him to close his eyes. As I stepped towards the sofa, I placed my hand in his hand and then had him slowly lift the open side of my wrist to his nose. Stewart opened his eyes and was pleasantly surprised with a beautiful aroma of sweet scented perfume. That is right! I purchased a wonderful bottle of perfume to model. I felt like a whole new world had been born right before my eyes (and nose). I was ready for any new adventure that Stewart and I could share together.

Friendship is a foundation for relationship

A DREAM ENCOUNTER

**Stewart Halfacre** *is a life-long resident of Dayton, Ohio. He attended Dayton Public Schools and is a 1979 graduate of Patterson Cooperative High School. Stewart (whose nickname is STU) received an Associates degree from Sinclair Community College (1981) and a Bachelors degree from the University of Dayton (1984) in Graphic Design. He enjoys walking, running, cooking, photography and spending time with his family.*

# When I Met Stephanie
## Uncovering the "mystery woman"

My life could be described as "Happy - Go - Lucky". God has always watched over my family and I even if sometimes I was unaware. The formative years were very pleasant as I replay the 1960s and 1970s in my mind. Those decades have melted away except for the images that entertain nostalgic trivia with my memory. Even if my recollection is not quite accurate about a certain past event, I always have a sense of contentment and happiness concerning my childhood. We had a small family that consisted of my Dad, Mom, brother (Vincent) and myself. Vincent and I shared some of the same artistic and music talents that allowed us to participate in many activities together. We were good friends who understood each other. My Mom always said we were psychic twins. Sometimes she would take us aside separately and asked us to pick clothes out of a catalog for one another. Each time, with almost 100%

accuracy, we would pick the same exact item on the same page. While at the University of Dayton, I took a Philosophy class that Vincent had taken the previous school semester. The professor was amazed that I selected the very same seat, even though I was unaware of where my brother sat or even that he took the same class. We were close.

Although I would illustrate my childhood as happy one, there were a few times when the picture was not perfect. My Mom and Dad separated when I was about nine years old. It was for the best because my parents were not getting along and their decaying relationship affected the atmosphere of the entire house. In 1969, it was very common (especially in our neighborhood) for woman to stay at home and raise their children, but my Mom as a result of the separation had to go back to work. This was just before the 1970s and all of our friend's mothers did not work outside the home. It was just as uncommon to live in a separated or divorced home. I can remember one of my friends saying, "Your Daddy ran away from your Mommy."

There was definitely a social stigma attached to homes without two parent's decades ago. I believe there was only one television show in the 1960s, "Julia", that addressed a single parent household. Single parent homes were perceived as different, chaotic and without discipline. Vincent and I were given freedom but with an understanding of boundaries and rules. We were not perfect but I believe in most cases, we had more discipline than most of our friends who had both parents at home. My Mom always said that one good parent is better than two so-so parents. She did an excellent job of raising my brother and I in a loving home without Daddy. Our lives were stable to a maddening degree. We lived in the same house, went to one elementary school and one high school our entire childhood. The stability was not boring. Stability gave us great peace and a sense of belonging especially after Mom and Dad broke up. We were connected.

Without a little risk, humans are destined to a stale existence with little chance of growth or opportunity. In November

of 1992, I was living a life of routine beyond extraordinary proportions. Work, work, and more work. Sometimes I would compile as many as 70 hours of work in a work week. I really enjoyed my job as a graphic designer. Ever since I was a child, I always enjoyed anything related to art, especially if it involved any kind of drawing. My father was a Technical Illustrator at Wright Patterson Air Force Base and I was never very far from his drawing table, which was usually covered with drawings. My hobbies as a youngster had materialized into a full-time occupation complete with pay and benefits. The only one glaring issue was that my life was very methodical with no variety in any sense. I lived by myself in a big two story house with only the bark of my mixed Lab, Corey, to keep me company. On occasion, I would date in between all the

**Growing up in the 1970s —**
*My brother, Vincent (left) and our Mom.*

work hours, but no significant relationships ever developed. There was never a genuine connection. My heart desired a real change or strategy toward relationships. My co-workers were always trying to fix me up with someone they knew. Blind dates were scary in some aspects but also allowed a sense of non-attachment to any possible relationship. If the dates were bad, then I did not feel obligated because I did not choose this particular person. I could always blame the matchmaker, when it did not work out and almost 100% of time these dates resulted in "plane-nose diving" failure. Against the approval of some of my friends and co-workers I enlisted the help of the Personal Ads. You know the ads in which most people are known to stretch the truth about themselves especially concerning physical aspects and education. In essence, this was a blind date based upon a personal resume. At least in this case, I was making my own selection, even if it was a selection based upon exaggerated personal information. Maybe, I should have listened to my friends. The series of dates I went on in November of 1992 were nothing short of

catastrophic disasters. If it is true that everyone has a person specifically made for them, then I managed to find every person in the world not made for me. It is like putting a fish and cat together. Sure there is an odd curiosity, but eventually the cat will eat the fish. At the time, it was probably in my best interest and survival on earth to take a break from dating. I am certain my friends and co-workers were exhausted listening to endless "train wreck" stories. There was a bright side. I was still breathing and my dog did not have any fleas.

In late December of 1992, all my co-workers had heard about my dating failures and given up on helping me. My abilities of persuasiveness had vanished along with the last bad date. I could not sell a coffin to a dead man. There were several question marks flashing in my mind. Was it easier for me to start a good relationship or catch a goldfish in the ocean? Odds were that I needed a fishing pole and some good bait. The task appeared to be daunting and extremely bleak. But sometimes we must try again until all possible avenues have

been exhausted. Success can be just a few feet from your last failure. What if I had given up while learning to ride my bike as a child? Do they make training wheels for a 200 pound grown man? It is not something you would wish to see, except maybe at a circus where clowns with big rubber shoes drive tiny small toy cars. In the real world, we have to get back up on the bike and try again without a safety net or the fake attachable nose. Reality has to make sense. Even after watching me crash and burn on several occasions, there was one co-worker who still had faith and was brave enough to shift through the mangled wreckage. Her name was Rosemary. I had worked with Rosemary for almost a year and found her to be very pleasant and positive. One day Rosemary asked if I was interested in meeting someone. She explained that her husband worked with a nice lady who was single. Wait a minute! This sounds like another blind date disaster waiting to happen. I was immediately hesitant, but at the same time I expected something wonderful because of Rosemary's great spirit. It seemed like a reasonable risk. So I asked Rosemary to get a phone number

via her husband. On January 3, 1993, I called Stephanie for the first time. I hardly ever used the phone unless I was ordering pizza. Just dialing Stephanie's number was a major event, because I have never been comfortable talking on the phone. Our conversation, which only lasted for a few minutes, was pleasantly friendly. Before saying goodbye, we arranged to meet the following Sunday afternoon for dinner. As I started the work week, my spirit filled with anticipation about seeing Stephanie in person. The only other time in my life I could remember that same feeling of excitement was on Christmas Day when I was a child. On Christmas Eve, I could hardly sleep without thinking about the surprises that were neatly hidden under the tree. My patience level was similar to that of a little kid's, but I had enough restraint or common sense not to show up at Stephanie's door at five in the morning. The wait for our "big date" was a little longer because Stephanie called

> **"There is more hunger for love and appreciation in this world than for bread."**
> ▪ Mother Teresa

to reschedule for the following Sunday. When January 17th finally arrived, it was a typical crisp winter day with deep blue skies and puffy clouds. Stephanie was brave enough to allow me to pick her up at her residence even though I was a stranger. I could have been a serial killer and now I know where she lives, or more likely a loser who now knows where she lives. Now I know possibly one of two things about Stephanie. #1) - she is completely crazy and would not care if a serial killer appeared at her doorstep or #2) - she is very careless. Stephanie's bravery actually stimulated my curiosity and added to the unexplainable excitement of the day ahead. As Stephanie opened the door, I was pleasantly relieved that she was from the planet Earth and not a creepy critter on the Sci-Fi channel. For a blind date, this is a very good start. She is not only attractive but she is very tall. First impressions are lasting and I was overwhelmingly stunned by Stephanie's beauty. We arrived at a local restaurant and were seated near the windows on the west side of dining area. The afternoon sun, which was rare on a winter day in January, playfully peaked through

large beautiful clouds and filtered through the window blinds. Billowing steam from chimneys on buildings nearby was the only indication of the freezing temperatures. This was not your typical winter day or typical blind date. On a blind date, the conversation usually is very awkward and strained. Talking to your dentist, with a mouth full of gauze, during an annual check-up would prove an easier task. Stephanie and I were as comfortable as old school buddies at a high school reunion. The conversation flowed in many different streams as we shared our experiences and goals for the future. Talking to Stephanie was like talking to a reflection of myself. We had much in our lives that was common and familiar. How do you know when you are comfortable with someone you just met? The

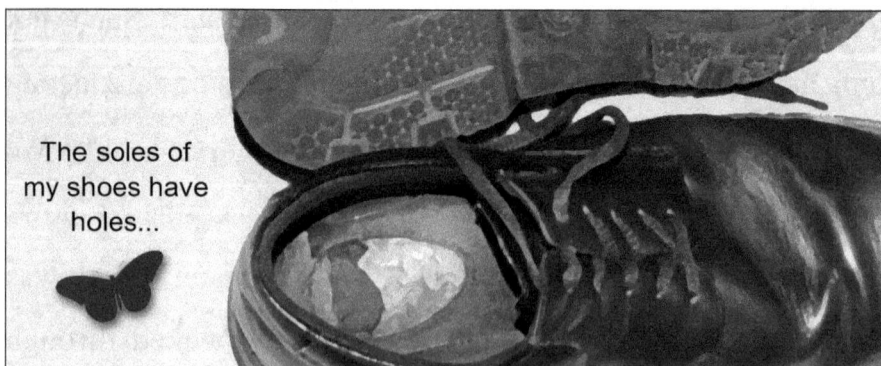

The soles of
my shoes have
holes...

answer is when you say, "The soles of my shoes have holes resulting in damp feet during rainfall." What would possess anyone to allow damaging confidential information to be shared with a stranger? It

> **"The difference between pretty and beautiful is pretty is temporal, whereas beautiful is eternal."**
> ▪ Unknown

seemed like I was programmed to sabotage the outcome of my date, considering my most recent attempts at a relationship were disastrous. Fortunately, Stephanie seemed to be amused by my "humbleness" or lack of quality shoe-ware. The good news was that the weather forecast did not include any liquid or frozen precipitation. I immediately knew that Stephanie's beauty emanated from her center and was not just a skin deep facade.

Stephanie was an intelligent person with a positive attitude toward life and was unlike any of my recent dates. As I drove Stephanie home and the wonderful afternoon came to an end,

I internally wished for a second date. Did I believe in love at first sight? Not really. My philosophy was that anything with worth or value took time to develop, including relationships. On television, we are constantly delivered the illusion or hallucination that two people can fall madly in love in a thirty minute program (including commercials). It is about the same amount of time it takes to make instant potatoes by just adding water. Some things in life do not require much thought but a meaningful relationship needs to be nurtured. In a Corvette, you can drive from 0 to 60 mph in a few seconds without breaking a bead of sweat, but a quality friendship requires real effort and commitment. Stephanie was an unique gem in a sea of common gravel. I was genuinely intrigued as I anticipated the opportunity to build a new friendship. Although it was only a brief encounter on a cold winter day, Stephanie's essence quickly echoed through my soul like a warm summer breeze blowing across the Gulf of Mexico. I felt connected.

FOLLOWING MY HEART

"Let your love be like the misty rains,

coming softly,

but flooding the river.."

— *Malagasy Proverb*

# *A* Commitment *of Love*
## The 8.8.8.8.10 Dream Reappears

Dreams can inspire you to go to the next level in your life and see a life ripe with abundance but without lack. On a few occasions I have had dreams where I was locked in a big scary building and someone or something was trying to harm me. While in the secluded realm of those moments of sleep, I learned quickly not to go to the dark cold depths of the basement. I always find myself going up to the highest possible level of the building and finding a safe hiding place with an open window to the outside world. Although some details of the dream include subtle differences each time, it always ends with me leaping out of the window and flying high above the puffy clouds away from my enemy. Sometimes in the realities of everyday life you may feel like there are no options, but we must commit ourselves to take a leap of faith and change the outcome. At this place in my life I look forward to new outcomes that flow outside of the familiar and this sometimes requires risk. I am not afraid to jump, because I know that when I make a leap, God will catch me.

1993 is only two months old but already generous with possibilities and transitions. As March began, I was looking forward to my trip to Europe to visit my brother and his family. Because I will be in Germany for almost three weeks, I have to make permanent living arrangements for my foster children, Shelly and Dawana. Although I loved my foster children very much, my new job made it difficult to address some of their special needs. I was sad, but I prayed for God to find them good caring homes. My prayers were answered in the next couple of weeks. Shelly was going back to live with her mother and Dawana was placed in the home of a local pastor and his wife. It was difficult, but I was confident in my heart that they would be alright.

The days in March were moving very rapidly. Maybe it was my anticipation for warmer spring weather or my excitement building around the trip to Germany. I had started the difficult task of packing clothes that have to last three weeks. Not only did the packing concern me, but how would I carry luggage with so many clothes. It was a minuscule problem and my anxiety was probably nothing but nervous energy about the trip. It was the same feeling you get when you do anything for the first time.

On Saturday March 20th, (two days before my departure), Stewart came to my house to visit and wish me well on my trip. I always expected some kind of nice surprise from my new friend and he did not disappoint me on this occasion. Our friendship was only two months old and I had already been spoiled. Stewart handed me a small 4 x 6 photo album. From the outside it looked like an ordinary album that you just put photos into but once I turned to the first page, I knew this was something very special. The first photo showed a sun-glassed clad Stewart holding up a black piece of paper with the letter "I". There were six more photos with the letters, L, O, V, E, U and an explanation point. It was like a photographic puzzle at first until I put the pieces all together and realize that the separate images spelled out I LOVE U! I think my heart just literally melted into my soul.

> **"It is easy to be brave from a safe distance."**
> ▪ Aesop

I was overwhelmed and touched by the beautiful message. In addition to the photographic message, Stewart also included various photos of us together (including one at dinner at his house). It was like a storybook of our friendship for the last two months and it made me smile because I knew this was a symbolic representation of real happiness. I think he really wanted to make sure I knew how he felt before our friendship went through a three-week separation. Stewart and I spoke to each other for several hours until we were both tired. As I began to walk him to the door, he wished me well on my trip and said, "I will see you when you get back."

On Sunday, (the day before my departure), Stewart called me with the sad news of his father passing away. His father had a massive heart attack sometime late Saturday night and died at home. I was sad for Stewart and told him I would pray for his family. Although, I never had the chance of meeting Stewart's father, I was thankful for my opportunity of meeting his son.

After saying goodbye to my daughter, Tia, who was staying with my parents, I was ready to board the plane to Germany with my youngest sister, Karen. This was my first trip to Europe and I was thankful to God for the opportunity of a trip that most people can not afford. It was a long trip, (almost 11 hours in the air), but I passed a lot of the time by reading, sleeping, or peaking out of the tiny windows. Occasionally, I would daydream and my mind would joyfully produce thoughts of Stewart.

As the plane finally touched down in Germany and our brother Mark greeted us, I realized how my life had transformed in just a few years. It was only a short time ago, that I could barely buy a pair of bargain basement shoes and now I was enjoying a vacation half-way around the world! I was grateful and I made every effort to experience everything Europe had to offer. There was nothing familiar about the surroundings. It was so alien to me I could have been an earthling visiting Mars. We visited various museums, castles and wineries. My biggest fear of Germany was the food and what would I be able to eat? I did not want to starve or be hungry on vacation, so I tried every morsel that was put on my plate. It was a smorgasbord of foods I did not recognize, but I enjoyed every bite. The entire trip was wonderful also because I got to spend time with my brother and his wife, Marion. Sometimes right before I went to bed, I would think about my daughter, Tia. Three weeks was the longest time I had been away from my little girl. It was always nice hearing her sweet voice on the few occasions when I was able to call home. I also missed Stewart too and was able to talk to him briefly on the phone only once because long distance calls from Germany to Dayton, Ohio were very expensive. It was wonderful talking to my friend, even though it was only for a few minutes.

It was a great three weeks in Germany, but I was ready and

eager to return to the familiar surroundings of my home. The flight home seemed much shorter because I was anxious to see Stewart. I wondered if he would be waiting for me. When I arrived at the airport in Dayton, my parents and little girl happily greeted me. It was great to see everyone, I was exhausted after the long plane flight and just wanted to crawl into bed. About one hour after I arrived home to relax, the phone rang and it was Stewart. He wanted to come to see me, even though there was a vicious thunderstorm filling the dark skies with an amazing light show as we talked. I was deathly afraid of thunderstorms, so I would have understood if he did not come out in the bad weather — but he really wanted to see me. In about ten minutes, Stewart arrived at my door with his usual "light knock" and smile. We were happy to see each other after three long weeks.

During the next several months, Stewart and I spent a lot of time together. We were getting to know each other while developing a very good relationship. Sometimes, Stewart would fix dinner for me and they were usually meatless meals since he was a vegetarian. The meals were good even though it was like eating a hamburger bun without the hamburger. Brownies was one of Stewart's specialties and he would often share brownies with Tia and me.

It was August and 1993 had evaporated faster than any previous year that I can remember. Maybe it is because of my trip to Germany or maybe because I was content and happy with my life. During one of our conversations, Stewart mentioned that his previous longest relationship lasted only eight months. In a few weeks, (the middle of September), Stewart and I would have known each other for eight months. What was he trying to tell me? Was he going to vanish when the clock struck eight months? Was he going to turn into a six-foot frog that eats giant flies?

## The first two 8s appear!

It was September 17th, exactly eight months from our very first date. My first immediate thought that danced in my head was, what does Stewart have planned? He had a flair for being creative and romantic at the same time. I had a drawer overflowing with beautiful cards as evidence. Other than being invited to his house for dinner, I had no idea what he was planning. My curiosity

> **"And now abide faith, hope, love, these three; but the greatest of these is love."**
> ▪ 1 Corinthians 13:13 (NKJV)

began building and simmered to a brisk boil. I was anticipating something magical! As I arrived at Stewart's house, I did not know what to expect. When I knocked on the door, all I could hear was the sound of my heart beating very rapidly. It was like a game show. Let's see what is behind door #1! Stewart slowly opened the door to reveal a romantic dinner made for two. He had also hung some pretty purple balloons alternating with gold streamers from the ceiling. My first thought was, all this to celebrate eight months? The dinner was good as usual and included homemade lasagna, salad and bread. Our conversation was enjoyable as usual, but Stewart reminded me again that his last relationship ended after eight months. I was not quite sure why he was so focused on a relationship that ended after a short time. Before I could complete one more thought in my head, Stewart smiled and handed me a medium sized gift box. I opened the box only to discover that there was a smaller box inside the first box. Finally, there was a third tiny box inside the second and I knew there was no way there was a tinier fourth box. I pulled the small piece of tape from the very small gift box to find a beautiful diamond ring inside. It's a ring! Stewart, who had been silent while I opened all the boxes, began to speak. He began to recite what a wonderful person I was and that the last eight months had been the best in his life. Stewart paused and smiled, and asked, "Will you marry me?" I smiled, (pausing briefly), and said, "Yes!" My senses were overwhelmed! Was I dreaming? This had also been the best eight months of my life. We built a great friendship together that had transformed into a great love. I think the both of us spent the rest of the evening just smiling, because we were very happy.

It had only been a few days since our engagement dinner and

I was still "intoxicated" with happiness. As I daydreamed about my future with Stewart, I began to recall the 8.8.8.8.10 dream that gave me chills eight years ago. It was like I heard a bell ring because I just discovered a revelation! I met Stewart eight years after the dream and now we were engaged after eight months. I was delirious with excitement because a pattern had been revealed. The dream that seemed like a foreign language to me was now within my understanding. It is a numerical pattern! I had never told Stewart about the 8.8.8.8.10 dream because he would probably think I was crazy and whacked out of my mind. The dream was meant specifically for me and would be revealed in God's time.

About a week after our engagement, Stewart and I decide to set a date for our wedding. I was am waiting patiently to hear what date he had in mind. Because of the pattern of the dream, I was convinced that May, 1994 was going to be the month he choose. May was eight months after our engagement. We had to stick to the pattern! Stewart cheerfully said, "How about

September 17, 1994?" No, pick May! I concealed my disappointment and asked, "Why September 17th?" He said it was exactly a year after we were engaged and he wanted to make sure his relationship with my daughter was good.

**September 17, 1993 —**
*Our Engagement Day!*

So, I said, "What do you think about May 7, 1994?" Even though Stewart thought May was too early to plan a wedding, he tried to keep me happy and entertains my alternative.

I was excited because I could see the next "8" forming, but that excitement was soon tempered by disappointment. We made several phone calls over the next few days to reserve a church and reception hall for May and every place was already booked. My heart literally left my body, because I was convinced that we were suppose to get married in May. I still did not reveal the dream to Stewart and eventually agreed to September 17, 1994 as our wedding date. I was still wondering about the dream and when the next "8" will occur. Although my curiosity was elevated to a delirious pitch, I still had faith to wait on God.

Over the next several months, Stewart and I enjoyed spending time together planning our big event. Our tastes were very similar and we decided on a black & gold color scheme. In December we went shopping and Stewart found some dresses for the bridesmaids. The dresses were long black sexy evening gowns with a long slit. I probably would have not selected these dresses a few years ago, but I had grown to appreciate Stewart's tastes in clothing and liked his choices.

Early the following year, I was on a lunch break with my co-worker and stumbled upon a little dress shop downtown. As I slowly browsed the clothing racks, I saw a dress that captivated my eyes and imagination. It was a beautiful gold beaded gown that had a v-neck front, halter back and slits on both sides. It was something Stewart would like and it was the perfect companion to the bridesmaid's dresses. It was not your traditional wedding gown. When I tried on the dress I felt like a queen in extravagant gold fabric. The dress was form fitting and wrapped my body like a glove — it was a perfect fit. There was not an inch available for alterations.

Planning a wedding, especially for someone with a full time job, was sometimes difficult. Sometimes the plans were also knocked off track. This process really taught me to be flexible. In February, my future mother-in law's pastor, (Rev. Frank Titus), had agreed to officiate at our wedding, but unexpectedly died in April of a sudden heart attack. In May, the month I wanted to get married, we discovered that the church chosen for our wedding was closing due to financial reasons. The passing of Rev. Titus saddened us. I did not panic, but for a short time we did not have a pastor or church for our special day. Things did eventually get back on track. Rev. Kathy Robinson, a friend of Rev. Titus, agreed to marry us at the church where she was the pastor. The church, (Grace United Methodist Church), was a beautiful 19th century giant stone structure. It was a perfect place for a fairy-tale wedding, because it reminded me of an European castle.

**I thought this was suppose to be an "8"...**

When May 7th, the day I wanted to get married, arrived on the calendar, I was very happy it was not our wedding day. Even though it was the middle of spring, the weather was more like winter. It was a cold, damp, foggy and very dreary day.

Although it seemed like every single minute of the day was dedicated to the wedding, we found time to spend with Tia. In June we went on weekend trip to an aquarium amusement park, along with one of Tia's friends. Later during July, Stewart took Tia and her cousin Leonard to the Moraine Airpark to get a ride in a single-engine plane over south Dayton and the Great Miami River. I knew Stewart would be a good father figure to Tia, because he genuinely enjoyed her company.

Now I know why wedding coordinators get paid well.

Planning an event is tedious work! Though there had been a million details to complete, I had enjoyed every second of constructing the wedding day with Stewart. We had learned some things that were unfamiliar to both of us, like dance lessons at a local dance studio. We didn't want our two left feet to be obvious during the first dance. Also, Stewart was using his artistic skills to create the flowers for all the bridesmaids and junior bridesmaids. Although it was his first time at making floral arrangements, the flowers were beautiful and cleverly echoed the color scheme of the wedding.

Also during the month of July, Rosemary, our matchmaker, informed us that she was pregnant. This was good news for her and Charles. The bad news was that Rosemary could not fit her (sexy) bridesmaids dress anymore and thought maybe she should pull out of the bridal party. We would not even consider leaving Rosemary and Charles out of the wedding because they were the reason Stewart and I met each other. Stewart was disappointed that the dresses he selected are now out of the wedding, but he was pleased with the solution. One of the sexy bridesmaid dress did survive, and it would be worn by my sister Karen who was the maid of honor. All the other bridesmaids were understanding and agreed to rent a new dress from a local bridal shop. Despite the fact that everything did not go as planned, all things surrounding our wedding were perfect to me.

It was September 16, 1994, the day before our wedding and all the planning was finally done. There was nothing left to do but marry Stewart. In the evening, my future mother in law gave us a rehearsal dinner at her church, Residence Park United Methodist Church. The food was good as well as the company. I was introduced to several members of Stewart's family who came to town to attend our wedding. As the dinner came to an end, all my thoughts were about tomorrow and all the good things God had planned for us. I was not nervous

**"Never run after a bus or a man. There will always be another one."**
▪ Old Irish expression

or anxious and knew Stewart was the right person for me.

The day was finally here! It was September 17, 1994 and I was getting married! Although, the day started with clouds and a brief shower, all the rain quickly dissipated to reveal a pleasant day with mild temperatures and an abundance of sunshine. Our ceremony was filled with many elegant touches, including a harp/flutist duo and local jazz singer Sandra Rutledge. Sandra's beautiful full-bodied voice injected the atmosphere with a soulful spirit that help set the tone for the rest of the day. The entire ceremony which was conducted without a hitch was full of happiness, love, laughter and everything we had envisioned. It went well because we were blessed with

My bridal bouquet...

the service of Mrs. Dora Crosby, a friend of Stewart's Mom. Mrs. Crosby served as our wedding day coordinator and made sure that the ceremony and reception was orchestrated with perfection. When things were not quite perfect we would just laugh. During the lighting of our unity candle, we could not get the wick to light. We could have drenched it with gasoline and it still would have been without a flame. Anyone else may have gotten upset, but we, (including, the minster), all had a good laugh and continued with the ceremony. A burning twenty dollar piece of wax was not important to us. Our unity was strong because of our commitment to each other.

*Love is not perfect but it is always true.*

THE PROCESS OF HEALING

"Out of difficulties

grow miracles."

— *Jean de la Bruyer*

# God's *Promise* is TRUE
## The journey to the third "8"

As we arrived at the wedding reception hall and stood in the receiving line, I was filled with an overwhelming sense of happiness because I knew God had blessed our union. My memories of the darkness that surrounded my life almost nine years ago was now just like a tea kettle vapor that had evaporated away. I was living a dream within a dream and the mysterious 8.8.8.8.10 dream that God gave me was clearly becoming a defined direction for my life. So far I know the first "8" represented my first meeting with Stewart, eight years after the dream. The second "8" materialized when Stewart and I were engaged eight months later. Although my excitement had reached a boiling point, I must wait patiently to see what God had planned for me. I had to wait for the rest of the story. I really had no clue if the next "8" would appear in eight weeks, eight months, or eight years. It was still a mystery that was in the hands of the divine.

The reception was as beautiful and wonderful as the wedding. It was a joyous celebration complete with good food and dancing that was shared with family and friends including Stewart's grandmother and my grandfather who were both in their 90's. During the planning of the wedding, Stewart had seriously considered asking our guests to bring a covered dish to the reception. What? I was grateful that our reception did not become a backyard "family picnic" but an elegant event. Stewart and I enjoyed our first dance together flashing some of the fancy dance steps we learned in our lessons prior to the wedding. When the last few guests left, Stewart and I were exhausted. We were very happy about our day that was the beginning of the rest of our lives.

Early Monday morning while the sun was still rising Stewart and I drove to the Dayton International Airport to debark on our four day Caribbean honeymoon cruise. Prior to the wedding, we did most of the planning of our big day together, however I planned the honeymoon myself. I knew Stewart had traveled to a lot of places so I wanted to experience something that neither of us had done before. At first Stewart was not to excited about boarding a cruise ship and floating out in the ocean in the middle of nowhere. The only thing he knew about cruise ships was what he had seen on television. He was not excited about being confined to a tiny cabin or what he referred to as a floating jail cell. Although he probably exaggerated his apprehension about the trip, I knew he was happy to be celebrating our honeymoon together, no matter where the honeymoon took place.

The plane flight, especially as we approached Miami Florida, was breathtaking. While I peaked out of the tiny airplane window, I could see the beautiful scenery that included a green lush coast line and the deep blue Atlantic. When we arrived in Miami, we were met by the cruise line representatives that quickly escorted us through the airport terminal. As soon as we walked outside the terminal, we were welcomed with warm tropical air and a pretty view of tall palm trees. Miami was such a vivid paradise, I could have happily spent the entire time at the airport terminal. We boarded a chartered bus which took us on a short tour of South Miami while traveling to the cruise port. Our eyes were filled with the sights of giant skyscrapers, sports cars of every hue, and pelicans. After about one half hour on the bus, we saw a sign for the cruise terminal and soon we could see the huge smokestacks of several cruise ships. It was an amazing site I will never forget. We could not believe the size of these majestic vessels because they were taller and wider than anything we could have imagined. Once we stepped foot on to our cruise ship, we knew the next four days would be an unforgettable adventure. Stewart's fears of staying in  a "jail cell" on the ocean were soon washed away. Our cabin was more than big enough and comfortable for the voyage. Besides the great food and the stunning interior of the ship, the most amazing thing to us was the ocean. Neither one of us had ever experienced being in the middle of the

> **"The true peace of God begins at any spot a thousand miles from the nearest land."**
> ▪ Joseph Conrad

ocean. There are few words to describe the feeling of wonder that you get when you realize that there is no land visible in any direction. It can only be described as a spiritual experience. The ocean is so vast that even the giant cruise ship

**September 20, 1994 —** *Enjoying our honeymoon!*

we were on seemed like a grain of sand adrift in the desert. God's love and grace for us is larger than an infinite ocean.

We made a port of call in Cozumel, an island located east of the Mexican Yucatan in the Caribbean Sea. During our visit to Cozumel we went to a near-by beach which was lined with pristine white sand and clear blue water. The beach was lush with tons of palm trees and Stewart and I enjoyed walking from one end to other barefooted. It was a heavenly adventure! We were so immersed in our own world, at first we did not notice the nude sunbathers that littered the secluded end of the beach. Our honeymoon was memorable and magical. The honeymoon, which was like a fantasy, was incredible but we were ready to begin our "real life" together back home in Dayton, Ohio.

Back in Dayton, Tia and I began the task of moving into Stewart's two story house. The process of moving was hardly ever enjoyable, but this was fun because Stewart and I were building our future. Stewart clearly wanted Tia to feel at home and allowed her to pick one of the bedrooms upstairs that was available. It was the beautiful bedroom with a large closet that faced the east, so there was always warm sunlight in the morning. Tia also was allowed to pick out a new paint color for her walls. The paint color was a vivid bright pink and not a color I would have picked but this was Tia's new room in her new home. It was fun decorating our new home, which really needed a woman's touch. Stewart had a beautiful home but it was a man cave and very masculine. The house was an older home with large windows that were hidden by old dusty blinds. I was able to convince Stewart that curtains would brighten up the windows and purchased some ivory laced curtains which accented the natural wood frames. Although Stewart told me he would never purchase curtains, he was impressed with my interior decorating skills. I had just moved in but I felt like I had always been here. Several years before meeting Stewart, I had a dream about a house that resembled the house I am now living in. In my dream, I saw a big house with white pillars and a large front porch with a grand piano in the living room just like Stewart's. I was suppose to be here.

In October 1994, my grandmother, Sadie Wilson passed away after a long battle with Alzheimer disease. She was not able to attend our wedding and I was worried she would not be here when we returned from our honeymoon. Stewart and I prayed that God would keep my grandmother here long enough for us to see her again. I was grateful God gave me more time with her. My grandmother was a wonderful lady who lived a rich life. She would have liked Stewart because he was a caring and patient person who loved me.

Prior to getting married, I began to experience some health issues and I was diagnosed with extensive amounts of fibroid tumor growth on my uterus. In November I went to the doctor and it was determined after a biopsy that the tumors were benign. While I was relieved and thankful to God that the tumors were benign, I still had a decision to make concerning my health. My doctor told me I needed to have surgery and could either choose hysterectomy or myomectomy. A hysterectomy involves surgically removing the entire uterus, which meant I would not be able to have anymore children. Before the doctor could say another word, I told him immediately that having an hysterectomy was not an option because I knew my plans and dreams for the future involved having children with Stewart. I also wanted to give my wonderful Mother in-law, LaVerne, her first grandchild. The myomectomy procedure involved removing the fibroid tumors from the uterus. Although the myomectomy would allow me to have the children, the fibroid tumors would probably grow back. At age 33, I was not ready for a hysterectomy and the thought of never having children again

> **"For she said, "If only I may touch His clothes, I shall be made well."**
> ▪ Mark 5:28 (NKJV)

was unimaginable. I felt like the woman in the bible who had the issue of blood and suffered a slow hemorrhage for 12 years. The woman believed if she could just touch the hem of Jesus's garment, she would be made whole. Through faith I also believed I could reach out to God and be healed.

In December I had the myomectomy procedure done to remove the fibroid growths and the surgery was successful. Since the recovering time lasted several weeks, I had a lot of time to meditate and pray about healing my body. On days when I was alone, I would occasionally daydream and imagine being pregnant. My mood was positive and I was anxious to finish my recovery time so Stewart and I could plan on having children. I wanted to just turn the pages of the calendar to the last day of my expected recovery.

As each day passed, I could feel myself healing and getting better. Early in January of 1995, I was laying in bed reading and praying when I heard a voice. The voice, which was very clear, said, "You will conceive eight months from the time you were married." Immediately my soul was filled with overflowing joy, because I knew God had just delivered another piece of the 8.8.8.8.10 puzzle. This was the third "8". For over nine years I have not told anyone about my dream, including Stewart. There were many times when I wanted to share the details of God's vision with him, but I feared he would think I was loony tunes. I knew Stewart believed in God, but I was not sure he would believe that I was visited by God in a dream like Joseph was in the bible. This sounded like something from the page of a story fictionalized by a Hollywood screenwriter. The question was where do I start. Revealing my prophetic dream was not something you casually share with someone but Stewart was not someone. He was the love of my life. As

I began to describe the dream where God spoke to me, I was not sure if Stewart was amazed or in disbelief. It had been two years since we had met, and by now he knew my relationship with God was real and that I would not make up some fantasy. I think that Stewart also realized that this amazing journey also involved him and our future family. It was our destiny together.

In late January I went to my follow-up doctors appointment. Usually I am not a big fan of going to the doctor but I was excited because I knew that the report would be good. This is going to be the day that Stewart and I can start making plans to get pregnant. After my examination, the doctor looked confused and puzzled. He explained that something had gone wrong during my recovery time and that both of my fallopian tubes had collapsed. Stewart and I really did not expect this kind of news, because my recovery had gone reasonably well without any complications. How could this be possible? Although, I was disappointed and felt like someone had sucker-punched me in my belly with a massive heavy brick, I knew what God had promised. My doctor told me not to worry and that there was a simple and painless procedure that could be performed to open my fallopian tubes.

A few days later I went back to my doctor's office to have the procedure performed this time without Stewart, who had to go to work. The procedure, which the doctor described as painless, involved injecting dye through the fallopian tubes. As the doctor began the procedure, I was very anxious and nervous. I just wanted to get done and go home. After several seconds I closed my eyes and tried to relax while I laid on the uncomfortable cold steel table. My state of relaxation was only temporary, because soon my eyes were ripped wide open by a terrible sharp pain. The simple procedure had turned into a complicated act of torture. Before my doctor could tell me, I knew that the procedure had failed. The spirit of disappointment was just as heavy as it was a few days ago, but this time I was miserable because of the pain. The pain was so deep, I had trouble focusing on what the doctor said. It was like his mouth was full of giant marbles. My heart sunk when I realized the doctor said that he would have to try the procedure again in a couple of months. Although I was hurt and upset, I continued to focus on my faith and trust in God. God always answers my prayers. Walking to the car to leave the doctor's office was difficult because of the sharp pulsating pain near my pelvis. Now, I was having second thoughts about driving myself to the procedure. As I drove down Salem Avenue, a very busy thoroughfare, all I could do was cry. The pain was so extensive it affected my concentration while driving and I finally realized that I had gone through an intersection and ran a red light. During this time of day there are usually cars lined up at this particular crowded intersection. This could have been disastrous, but God was watching over me during my lapse of attention. When I finally arrived back home safely, I thanked God for his mercy.

During the next couple of months, I continued to recall what God had told me in January. I was confident and believed I would get pregnant in May, eight months after my marriage to Stewart. While my body was still in the process of healing, I was encouraged by my faith. Almost everyday I would read a certain bible scripture that states, "Whose report will you believe?" As these words began to settle in my heart, my soul's response was like the refrain of an old gospel song, "I will believe the report of the Lord!"

As warm springtime weather and April arrived, we were encouraged by the good news of our matchmaker friends, Charles and Rosemary. They are now the proud parents of their miracle twins, Sophie and Joseph. After twelve long years, their hope of being parents had finally been realized in the arrival of a girl and boy. Stewart and I are were happy for our friends and were reminded of the power of prayer and hope. We knew and believed that sometime in the near future that our prayers would be answered and our hope would prevail.

In the next couple of weeks I would be going back to my doctor to have the procedure to open my fallopian tubes. Although the painful experience was still lurking in my memory, I was excited because this time it would be successful. On Easter Sunday, April 16, 1995, I remember sitting in the choir stand because I was the choir director. As usual it was a very crowded Easter service. My father, who was the pastor, preached a good message and called people up for prayer who needed a healing. I had been in the prayer line a couple weeks ago, and I did not want the added attention, so I decided to stay seated because my miracle healing was already claimed. Once again, my father asked for people to come up to the altar for prayer, but this time it was a little different. He said God is speaking to someone here and all you have to do is get in the prayer line and receive your healing. This time I was not reluctant and got in the prayer line to receive my healing. The warm healing touch of Jesus soothed my soul almost instantaneously. I was healed!

It had been almost three months since the failed procedure and now it was time to try again. Once again I was at the doctor's office, (this time with Stewart), trying to get comfortable on that cold steel table. As I relaxed and the doctor began to perform the procedure, I noticed something different from the previous time. There was no pain. This had to be a good sign considering I practically crawled away crying in severe agony the last time. After a few minutes, which seemed more like an hour, the doctor said the procedure was successful and that we could plan to get pregnant. Stewart and I were so filled with joy when we left the doctor's office, we could have floated away like over-inflated balloons. God's grace and promise is always true.

### The third "8" has arrived!

Late in May 1995, just as God had promised, I became pregnant eight months after Stewart and I were married.

*God can replace your tears with joy!*

SEEDS TO BLOSSOMS

"When you're finished changing,

you're finished."

— *Benjamin Franklin*

# *Birthing A* DREAM
## Living in the Vision

It had only been a few days and the news of my pregnancy had created an indescribable anticipation for Stewart and I. The amazing happiness had brightened every inch of our daily lives. Every second of the day was occupied by thoughts of whether our blessing will be a little boy or girl. Although it was very early, we had started to choose baby names. If we have a little boy, he would be named after Stewart's brother Vincent and if it was a girl, her name would be Maria in honor of my Mother. I planned to enjoy every little thing about the pregnancy for the next nine months.

In early June I began to rapidly gain weight and realized this pregnancy was very different than my first one with Tia. When I was pregnant with Tia, it took me months to gain an ounce of weight and even longer to show. I thought it was just my excitement and imagination at first, but the button on the waistline of my pants never lie. I had gained a lot of weight in the first couple of weeks. In my own personal experience the only other time I heard about a quick weight gain early in a pregnancy was last year when my friend Rosemary told me she could not fit into her bridesmaid dress. When I saw Rosemary a few weeks later, I told her she was carrying twins and this was before she officially knew. For the second time in my life I was telling someone they were expecting twins and this time, it was me!

On June 15, 1995, Stewart and I went to the doctor's office for my first prenatal appointment. This was an appointment I was looking forward to. My doctor confirmed, what we had already discovered with a store bought kit several weeks ago, that I was pregnant. The confirmation, although not a surprise, was still exciting to hear from the lips of my doctor. Now I had some news I wanted to eagerly tell my doctor. I believed, even though it was early in my pregnancy, that I was carrying twins. As I told my doctor, I could sense that he had heard this before many times from his excited pregnant patients. This reminded me of a little kid telling their father that they were going to grow-up to be an astronaut one

> **"It is said that the present is pregnant with the future."**
> ▪ Voltaire

day and the father would humor the child and say, "Okay honey, that is wonderful." The doctor's response was what I expected. He (humored me) and said it was too early to determine if I was pregnant with twins. It did not mater what he said, I knew what I believed. Before leaving, the doctor told us that the expected delivery date was February 15, 1996. I knew this date was just an educated guess. During my first pregnancy, I was given a date of July 26th and Tia was finally born on August 8th.

During the next couple of days, even though it was early, I began to tell friends and family that I was pregnant. My belly had taken on a new enlarged shape so rapidly there was no way to hide the obvious. My mid-section was like a yeast roll that had over risen the pan.

I dreamed almost everyday, some were ordinary snapshots but other dreams were unique and special full length movies and the only thing missing from these dreams was a large bucket of buttered popcorn. The next morning, I had a vivid and descriptive vision. I dreamed I was at a garage sale looking for baby items. There was a large maze of baby items for sale that were neatly organized together. As I began to look through the long tables, I saw two highchairs, two t-shirts, two bibs and two strollers. It was a smorgasbord of everything you needed for a baby, but it was all categorized in sets of two's. While I was looking at the price tags, the lady who was selling the merchandise told me if I wanted anything, it had to be purchased in sets of two. When I woke up, I knew the feeling in my spirit had just been confirmed literally by a lucid and specific dream delivered by God. I was going to have twins! I immediately shared the details of my extraordinary dream with Stewart who was excited but obliviously overwhelmed by the revelation. After hearing the instant replay of my dream, Stewart, who was a quiet person, was almost mute even by his standards. Maybe he was concerned about the expense of buying the huge mounds of diapers or maybe it was the fear that he might have to change an endless supply of dirty diapers. The diapers were a small detail in a big adventure that was going to permanently change our world.

The whole idea of twins had settled into every tissue of my over active brain. I started to wonder if I would have two girls, two boys, or a boy & a girl. Although any combination would be wonderful, I was intrigued by the thought of having a boy and a girl. It would be wonderful to have a boy for Mommy and a girl for Daddy. I have always wanted a little boy, because little boys grow-up to be young men that take care of their Mommy. Once again I started to look for baby names and I had already made up my mind that a boy would be named Vincent but I also wanted a girl's name that would be compatible with Vincent. It had to be a name that started with the letter "V". We tried several names like Valencia, Venita, Valerie and Vanetta but none of the names flowed when we pronounced them out loud with the name Vincent. Stewart finally said, "How about Vincent and

Victoria?" I immediately loved the name Victoria and I could actually hear myself calling Victoria by her nickname, Vickie.

As the month of June began to come to an end, I had another dream featuring twins. The dream two weeks ago revealed that I was carrying twins. This dream was like having an ultrasound while asleep because it uncovered the sex of the babies. In my dream I saw two girls with very long hair playing together in separates beds that were set up along one side of a wall in the bedroom. It is obvious that the girls are very happy and physically active. One of the girls was able to scale the sides of her bed with precision so she could climb into the other bed with her twin. When I finally opened my eyes, I knew this dream was a glimpse into the future. Although I was happy to see two healthy girls, I was also upset about the long hair because I am not a hair expert.

> **"Tigers die and leave their skins; people die and leave their names."**
> ▪ Japanese Proverb

When Tia was little and I had my foster girls, combing several heads of hair was a daily struggle. You would think my hands were composed of all thumbs because I could not manage hair to save my life. Eventually Tia, through self preservation, learned how to do her own hair to avoid hoards of laughter and public ridicule. With practice on my oldest foster daughter, Jessicah, I was able to become an adequate master of children hair-dos. The thought of combing and brushing two little heads was intimidating but I would have the luxury of Tia's styling expertise. Besides the sudden hair phobia, it was one of the most realistic and enjoyable dreams that I have ever experienced.

On July 5, 1995 while at work I began to experience pain and bleeding. I called my doctor who immediately scheduled me to see an ultrasound specialist early that afternoon. As Stewart drove me to the hospital, we began to pray and put our situation in the hands of God. We prayed for a normal pregnancy without any complications. When we arrived at the hospital in the prenatal section, we were taken to a small room which was very sparse and sterile. The only decor was a table, a couple of chairs, and an ultra sound machine. After I changed into the standard hospital gown, Stewart and I waited for several agonizing minutes for the ultrasound technician. Even though we only waited 10 minutes it seemed like it was an eternity before the ultra sound technician and an assistant finally walked into the room to start the examination. I was a little anxious and nervous as the technician smeared a jelly like liquid all over my round belly. Stewart and I intently watched the little ultrasound monitor that produced abstract black and grey moving images. We had no clue what the images were. They could have shown us photos of a moon landing and we would have not known any difference. After several minutes, the medical assistant and technician reviewed the ultrasound images and mumbled a few words between themselves. The medical technician turned and faced us and said, "You possibly came here for bad news, but I have some good news, congratulations, you are pregnant with twins!" Our emotions went from cautiously concerned to abundantly ecstatic in the same amount of time it took to breath a quick sigh of relief. God answered our prayers. The abstract ultrasound images became realistic as the medical personnel began to identify the two distinct fetuses. The feeling in my spirit and the dreams I recently experienced about the twins had been corroborate by ultrasound technology.

We thanked God that the pregnancy and my health were normal. Real life definitely was not normal as we looked forward to the extraordinary birth of our twin blessing. The next day I continued my "normal" daily routine and went back to work, although I admit my mind was preoccupied for the rest of the week. I struggled to get anything done. In the evenings, Stewart and I would go for walks to help with my fitness during the pregnancy. I needed to stay active so I could carry the babies as long as possible, since twins have a tendency to be born early. We started the habit of walking together before we were married. It would always give us private time alone to share things about our day. Walking together has not only kept our bodies healthy but our relationship as well. Our walks are now filled with talks about preparation for the twins.

The next couple of months can be described as the days of metamorphosis, as my body took on new proportions that I did not even experience during my first pregnancy. A lot of my clothes had become too tight. My body had developed a temporary amnesia to everything I wore. When I looked in the closet, my clothes looked familiar but they did not recognize me. It was time to get some clothing that would fit my expanding oval frame. Women do not usually enjoy buying larger clothing but this was another enjoyable part of the pregnancy for me because I also needed comfortable clothes to wear to work. During my big shopping trip, Stewart helped me find several dresses and a blue polka dotted maternity swimsuit. Although it was

> **"The light of the eyes rejoices the heart, And a good report makes the bones healthy."**
> ▪ Proverbs 15:30

summer and it was blazing hot, I was not sure when I would get the chance to wear a swimsuit, but it was a fun thing to have.

The weather in August of 1995 was the usual summer time smoker in Ohio. I preferred warm weather to the icy cold, but the heat sometimes made me uncomfortable during my pregnancy. For some reason, I always felt hot from the inside out. It was like the babies were roasting marshmallows inside my belly. The only way to relieve that internal camp fire was to guzzle lots of water. Sometimes I would drink a gallon of water a day. During a hot day in August of 1995,

**Early pregnancy —**
*Putting on the pounds fast!*

along with many family members we traveled to a local water amusement park to celebrate Tia's 11th birthday. This was my chance to wear my fashionable polka dotted maternity swimsuit and cool off in a pool of refreshing cold water. I walked to the shallow end of the wave pool lowered myself waist high in the water and closed my eyes. The water was so soothing with my eyes closed I daydreamed that I was in the glistening blue Caribbean Ocean. It was the same relaxed and spiritual sensation I experienced on our honeymoon. This was a very relaxing and pleasant excursion for me while I was pregnant. If I did not work, I would be here everyday soaking my ball shaped belly. It was a beautiful day and Tia enjoyed her birthday celebration with her cousins.

While I continued to grow and the calendar days quickly melted away, I sometimes thought about the 8.8.8.8.10 dream. I was still waiting patiently on God to tell me what the last 8 & 10 would mean for me and Stewart. Earlier I made the mistake of trying to guess what the dream meant without waiting for God. God always does things in his own time and we are on his clock, not the other way around.

On September 17, 1995, Stewart and I celebrated our first wedding anniversary. It had been a wonderful and interesting 365 days together. The best part of our relationship was that we really enjoyed sharing each other's desires and dreams. We also liked to make each other laugh at the strangest things as we had discovered throughout our union and especially during the week of our anniversary. On the day of our wedding, I had my Mom store the top of our wedding cake in her freezer with the intention of un-thawing it a year later for Stewart and I to eat. Stewart, who generally does not eat cake more than 24 hours old, was emphatic that there is no way that cake that was frozen for a year would be edible for human consumption. Contrary to Stewart's "moldy after a day" cake theory, I have had one year old anniversary cake before and it was very edible. After our cake was removed from Mom's freezer and thawed, we each got a fork and prepared to sample a delicious bite of cake. As the icing melted and slid down our throats we both looked at each other as the flavor left an odd bitter after taste. Our anniversary cake for some reason tasted like fish. Apparently, my Mom forgot the cake was in the freezer and accidentally stored fish on top of it, which resulted in what we called the "fish cake". Stewart laughed and said, "I told you the cake would not be any good in the freezer that long." I was looking forward to that cake,

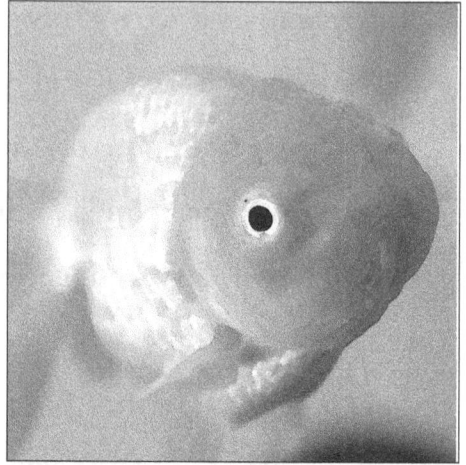

**September 17, 1995 —**
*A "fish cake" anniversary — yummy!*

especially since I had only a few baby nibbles of the actual wedding cake. A few days later, Stewart told me he had a surprise for me in a box he brought home after work. Before I could get one corner of the box open, Stewart began to giggle. Now I was a little hesitant, but I finally got the box open to see a two-layered white cake decorated with plastic fish. It was hilarious and sweet at the same time. I laughed so hard it made my belly hurt and it did not take much for my stomach to feel uncomfortable in my pregnant state. We always found ways to laugh and that is what I have enjoyed about our relationship.

In early October, Stewart and his brother Vincent began to work on the baby nursery in the empty bedroom to the right of the master bedroom. The room needed a lot of work, mainly repair of a old plaster ceiling that had cracked and fallen leaving a big hole near the light fixture. The room was in such bad shape I really could not envision what it would look like when the remodeling was completed. In just a few days Stewart and Vincent removed all the loose plaster and installed a new drywall ceiling. The space was transformed from an old room in disrepair to a beautiful future nursery for our babies in less than a week. The only thing left to do was add a fresh coat of paint and new carpet. When I closed my eyes and thought about how seemingly non repairable the room was just a short time ago, it reminded me of the human experience. Even when we find ourselves in total chaos, God can take the broken pieces to construct a masterpiece.

As my stomach continued to grow like a pumpkin and the last few colorful leaves fell off the trees, Stewart and I drove to the next doctor's check-up appointment on a sunny autumn day late in October 1995. Although my body had already told me and everyone else, the ultrasound revealed that the babies were growing and developing well. We also were able to hear their strong individual

**Fall 1995 —**
*It looks like I swallowed a pumpkin!*

heart beats which sounded more like washing machine in wash mode. My doctor was happy with the progress of the babies, but a little concerned with my health because I had gained a lot of weight during the pregnancy. Stewart and I had continued our walking routine throughout the pregnancy, but due to the weight of the babies my walking was more like a duck's waddle. Because of my rapid weight gain, I was at risks for Gestational Diabetes and Pre-eclampsia (pregnancy induced hypertension), so the doctor suggested that I should go on partial bed rest in the next few weeks. The doctor also determined from the current size of the babies on the ultrasound an estimated due date of the first week of February 1996. As soon as Stewart heard February, his creative juices began to work overtime and focused on Groundhog Day (February 2nd). Stewart laughed and said the first baby would be born and see a shadow and that shadow would be its twin. He was already drafting Groundhog Day announcements in his mind. It really did not matter what the day the babies were born, we were just grateful to God that the pregnancy had gone well.

On Thanksgiving, my wonderful Mother in-law, LaVerne, prepared a delicious Thanksgiving dinner for us. I enjoy food, but it took a lot of effort for me in my current condition just to fix a sandwich and I needed a little more than a sandwich on "Turkey Day". I was very thankful on a day of thanks, that someone would take the time and pour themselves into cooking a homemade meal for us. LaVerne took a lot of joy in making other people happy whether it was family or friends. Now it is apparent where Stewart learned his good cooking skills and the added joy when he cooked for his family.

A week after Thanksgiving, as directed by my doctor, I took sick leave from my job to begin my days of partial bed rest to ensure my health and the health of the babies. Our two-story house only had a bathroom on the second floor. To keep me from walking or waddling the stairs, Stewart prepared my breakfast and also filled a cooler with lunch everyday prior to leaving for work. My thoughtful husband tried to make me as comfortable as possible but sometimes just laying in bed was difficult. It was like there was a big exercise ball squeezed up under my shirt. It is hard enough trying to roll on an exercise ball, now I was the exercise ball, but with a head, legs and arms. My time on bed rest was spent reading pregnancy books, watching soap operas and daydreaming about the birth of the babies. Occasionally the babies would entertain me by performing acrobatic stunts and flips in my belly. They were so active, it seemed like they were wrestling in a real knock down steel cage match. It was strange watching what appeared to be hands or feet push out my stomach in every conceivable cartoon like angle. Although I was enjoying the rest, I missed talking to my friends at work who would call me a couple times a week.

The month of December started with warmer than normal weather at 59 degrees. Anyone that has known me for a few seconds is aware of my dislike for ice, snow and cold weather. Just give me a tropical breeze and 85 degrees of warmth and I am in heaven. If I were a bear, I would hibernate in the late fall and all of winter. My doctor's prescribed bed rest gave me a legitimate excuse to stay inside up under the bed covers. Although the month started out mild and peaceful, December proved to be a chaotic and stormy period for my family and friends. Stewart's Mom, LaVerne, found out after a doctor's examination and test results that she had Thyroid Cancer which would require immediate surgery. A few days later, a co-worker called to inform me that a fellow friend and co-worker suffered life threatening injuries from a terrible traffic accident. During weekdays when I was alone in the peaceful silence of the house, I would always take time to pray and meditate. The best time to talk to God is in the peaceful silence when it is just you and him. After hearing the bad news, I spent the next several days praying for the miraculous healing of LaVerne and LeDon. On December 18, 1995, Stewart took his Mom to have Thyroid surgery. This type of surgery was routine and Laverne's procedure went well. Since LaVerne was going to be in recovery for a couple of hours, Stewart left the hospital with plans to return later. When Stewart returned later that afternoon, he discovered his Mom had been moved to the Intensive Care Unit. Apparently, something had gone wrong with the anesthesia which created a medical emergency with her respiration. What should have been routine now was not routine. This proved we can not

> **"God has two dwellings; one in heaven, and the other in a meek and thankful heart."**
> ▪ Izaak Walton

take anything for granted. Stewart called me from the hospital room and we immediately began to pray together. The next day the area experienced a heavy snowstorm that dumped several inches of snow overnight. Normally, you would not find me out in weather that produces anything that is white and fluffy or shiny and slippery but we needed to check on LaVerne at the hospital. I wanted to also visit LeDon and support him in his recovery. When I went to visit LeDon, although he was in bad physical condition, his spirit and attitude was very positive. He knew his road to recovery was very long, but he believed that he would overcome his injuries. LeDon was confined to a wheelchair, but he inspired me with his faith that God would fix his broken body. A day later, LaVerne's condition improved and she was taken off the breathing apparatus and moved to a regular hospital room. She eventually went home to recover after her unexpected extended stay. We were thankful about the recoveries of LaVerne and LeDon. God is good!

Late in December, we invited LaVerne over to our house for

dinner to celebrated the end of 1995 and the year to come.

As the New Year 1996 arrived, we were greeted with another heavy snowstorm on January 2, 1996. It was the same day that I had another ultrasound scheduled. I was glad Stewart navigated the messy roads to doctor's office. If I wanted to drive, it would be impossible because of the gigantic size of my tummy. There was no room for me to squeeze behind the steering wheel. Over the duration of my pregnancy I had gained 70 lbs pounds and top the scales at 209 lbs. Maybe it was a good thing that I was currently having trouble keeping food down. The latest ultrasound was still unable to determine the sex of one of the babies. We were positive one of the babies was a girl but are unsure of the other. Funny, they had not been born yet and already one of the twins was playing hide and seek. The great anticipation was building with only 30 days to the big event.

The winter of 1996 continued to be a long snowy event as another big snowstorm blanketed our area on January 6th through the 7th. Ten inches of pretty fluffy snow fell in a short period of time, which resulted in several church services being cancelled (including my father's church service). I could not remember my father ever cancelling a Sunday morning service in my life except during the blizzard of 1978. The streets were hazardous but from my bedroom window the snow was visually pristine and beautiful. During my couple months of bed rest, I enjoyed looking out my window into the rest of the world.

January 25, 1996 started like every other day since I was put on bed rest. Stewart went to work and Tia went to school, while I began my day by eating breakfast that Stewart had prepared for me. This had been a familiar ritual since last November. Early in the afternoon, right after the soap operas, I began to experience periodic pain and it felt a lot like labor pains. At first I was not concerned because over the past few months I had experienced a lot of aches and pains, even false labor pain called Braxton Hicks contractions. This pain was a little different. After about an hour of the pulsating pain, I decided to give Stewart a call to describe what I thought were labor pains. Stewart, who was addicted to every morsel of information in the pregnancy book, told me to look at the chapter on labor pains and start counting the time in between. The pain came every about 10 to 12 minutes consistently for the next several hours. The uncomfortable sharp pain in my lower back was like clock work. Stewart said we only had to worry if the pain was about 7 to 8 minutes apart "according to the book". I really did not want a page on in a book to determine whether I went to the hospital. Stewart decided to stay at work to get some work completed just in case we had to go to the hospital in the next couple of days. When he finally got home about 7:00 p.m., the pain, which was predictable over the last few hours, had become sporadic. Stewart wanted to count the minutes between the pains with me, even though the pains are not as severe or regular. I was exhausted and I just wanted to eat and go to bed. After seeing my painful expression, now Stewart was too nervous to go to bed and decided we should go to the hospital in case I was in labor. The closer we got to the hospital the least frequent my pain was occurring. After arriving at the hospital I was taken to an examination room and hooked up to a machine that measures contractions. Though the pain/contractions had seemed to stopped, the machine was showing that I was experiencing the start of labor. The hospital personnel took several more measurements and then made a phone call to confer with my doctor. My doctor recommended that I stay overnight in the hospital and scheduled a C-Section delivery for Friday morning. Because I really did not expect my doctor to keep me at the hospital, Stewart had to go home and get some clothes and personal items for himself, Tia and me. It was really difficult trying to sleep because I was too excited about finally giving birth to the twins. I do not believe anyone shut their eyes very long overnight. Early Friday morning, I was moved to another room and prepped for surgery where I was hooked up to an intravenous fluid for about an hour and a half. Any wait at this point seemed like a lifetime, because I was becoming increasingly anxious. The medical staff administered an epidural anesthesia injection near my spine that blocks pain and sensations during delivery. In about 5 to 10 minutes I began to feel numb from my chest down to my feet. I was not really sure, but some time had passed before I was moved to an operating room. They allowed two people to be present during the birth, so my sister Karen and of course Stewart joined me. Before they could join me, they had to wash their hands and put on surgical scrubs, which made funny looking outfits. Karen and Stewart were not out of place, because that is what everyone was wearing. As Stewart sat in a chair next to me, he was smiling, but I knew he was nervous. The nurses positioned a curtain/sheet right above my large pregnant belly, so I would not be able to see the doctors cut me open during the C-Section. The joyous moment finally arrived after all those months of carrying the babies and spending the last 60 plus days on bed rest. On January 26, 1996 at 9:42 a.m. the doctor delivered a baby girl, who we named Veronica. She was beautiful! Before I could catch my breath, two minutes later the doctor held up another beautiful baby girl, who we named Victoria. The girls in a non-stop flow of sheer joy and purpose completed each other in body and name. The name Veronica means "to bring victory" and while Victoria's name means "to be victorious". From 9:42 a.m. to 9:44 a.m., Stewart and I experienced the most euphoric high of our young marriage. We thanked God for our healthy wonderful miracles and the amazing opportunity to be parents of two precious little girls.

The pregnancy and delivery was hard on me physically and I spent several extra days in the hospital. Victoria was placed in an incubator in NICU due to some breathing difficulties. I finally saw Victoria for the first time on Sunday, two days after her birth. After six days, my physical health had improved and the doctor discharged me and the babies on a bitterly cold day, the last day of January. Stewart patiently squeezed two babies, two car seats and me into a car that now seemed very small. It was so cold the car barely got warm before we arrived at LaVerne's house. My sweet Mother in-law had graciously invited us to stay with her for a few days while I recovered. It was wonderful that the girls got to spend the first days of their life with their Grandmother.

## The fourth "8" & "10" are revealed and now the vision is complete!

While cooped up in the hospital bed I recalled and reflected on the 8.8.8.8.10 dream that I had experienced in 1986. I realized that the amazing vision that was "time released" in my life over the last several years was now complete. Prior to the birth of the girls I did not know what the last "8" and "10" would be and I did not want to second guess God. The amazing birth of the twins represents the rest of the story. On January 26, 1996, the girls were born eight months after they were conceived (the weekend of May 26, 1995). Their amazing birth happened ten years after I was given the dream that changed my life and the lives of my family forever.

A joyful life is better when shared

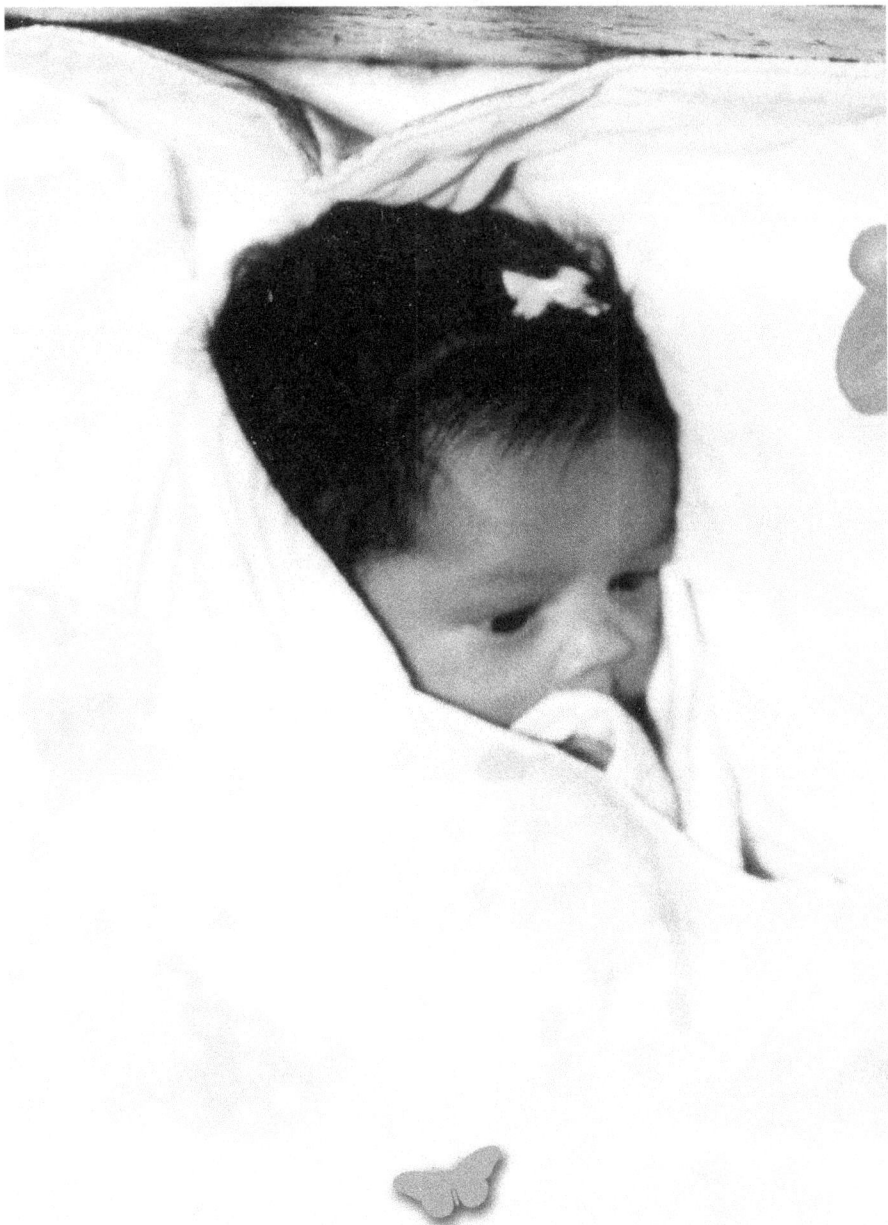

Veronica Renee Halfacre
— *Born January 26, 1996 • 9:42 a.m.*

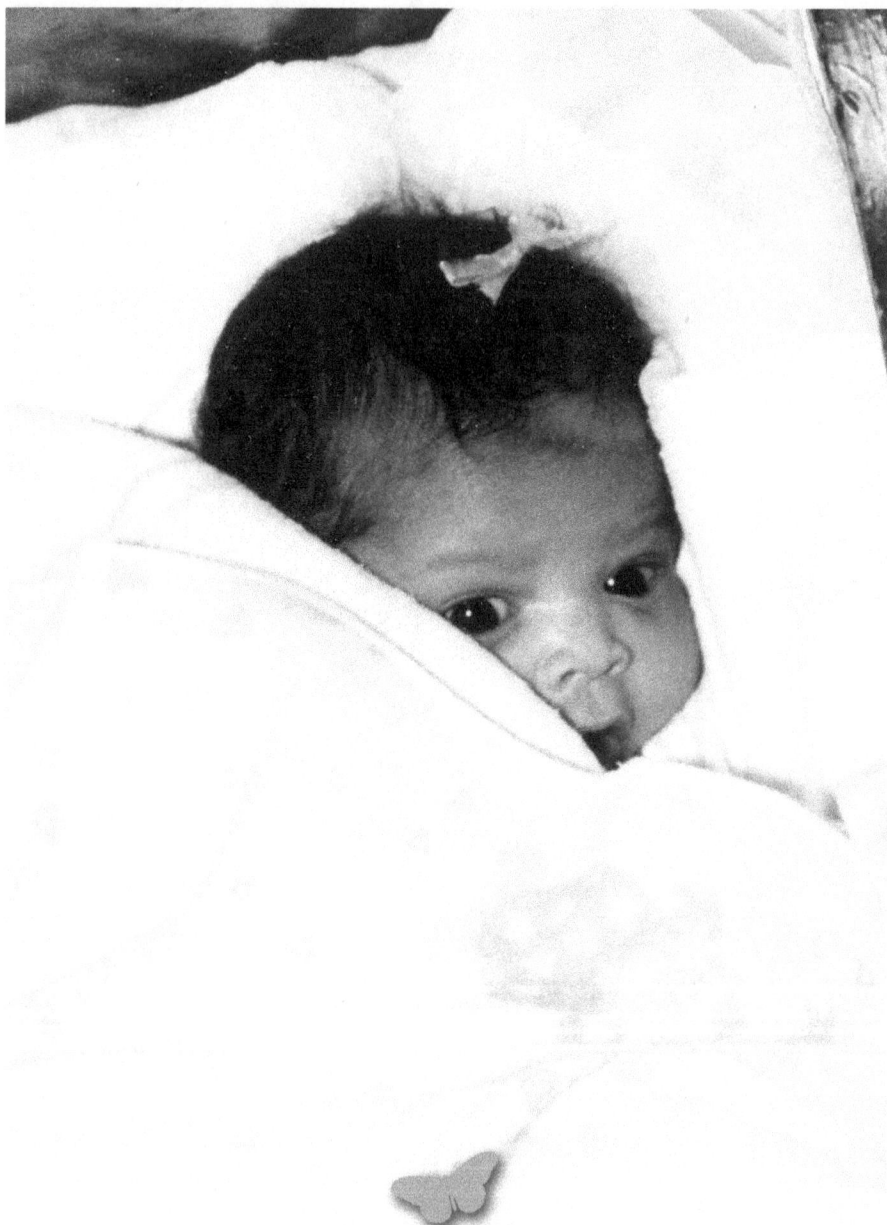

Victoria Anne Halfacre
— *Born January 26, 1996 • 9:44 a.m.*

THE LIFE OF ABUNDANCE

"Blessed is the season

which engages the whole world in

a conspiracy of love."

— *Hamilton Wright Mabie*

# A Season of BLESSINGS
## A retrospective of life after the DREAM

It is now 2011 and it has been 25 years since I experienced the life changing "8.8.8.8.10" dream. The vision from God was like a giant boulder that plunged into my soul, leaving ripples of perpetual blessings that are still in motion today. God's presence in my life has led to numerous opportunities, meaningful relationships and timely supernatural miracles. The dream was a blueprint to build the life I really wanted and desired. Unlike a blueprint for a house, this blueprint for life continues to build upon itself and create new possibilities. The following is an account of my life after the final piece of the dream was revealed with the birth of our twin girls.

### Life After the Dream

The birth of Veronica and Victoria marked the completion of the vision that God gave me, but also the beginning of a challenging and promising life ahead.

It was a joy and sometimes a challenge getting to know and raise the girls during their first year in the world. At the very beginning, I made the decision to breast feed my babies because I knew this was a good way to ensure a healthy start. While I was still at the hospital, Veronica and Victoria had difficulties adapting to breast feeding, but I did not give up and in a few days I had their feeding down to a smooth timely pattern. Although sometimes it became difficult during the early morning hours when I was sleepy and they were very hungry. The girls are not identical but looked very similar, so occasionally I was not sure which baby I had fed. I think sometimes the same baby was fed twice during a feeding. Stewart always joked that they were like little vampires because of their late night habits. Despite the sleep deprivation, my intentions were to breast feed for at least a year. As their little razor sharp teeth began to come in and they started to bite me, the breast feeding ended after seven months.

When I first met Stewart, it did not bother me that he only

attended church maybe four times a year (Easter, Mother's Day, Thanksgiving and Christmas). I knew he believed in God and that was all that mattered. After the girls were born, Tia and I would go to church every Sunday and carry the girls in their car seats up a steep set of steps. It was not easy carrying the girls and their diaper bags, but I wanted them to attend service with me. One Sunday, Stewart surprised me and decided to help me carry the girls and attend church. He began to attend church as a habit after that first time. I remember when Stewart testified in church that it was his 10th Sunday in a row and that he was enjoying service. It was funny that he was counting, but it was important to him because previously he was an occasional church attendee. Stewart was building a personal relationship with God and that was a good thing.

## A Year of Change and Transition

The new millennium started with fears of the Y2K virus and end of the world prophecies. We did not live in fear but in the knowledge and faith that God's word would always prevail and take care of us. The year 2000 was not the end but the beginning of changes for our family. God said he who finds a wife finds a good thing. The bible also says a woman is to follow her husband because he is the head of the family. A decision made by my husband would be the catalyst for a new direction spiritually.

During May of 2000, Stewart began watching a local minster's television church program. During the same time period, a co-worker, Bill Johnson, who attended this church invited us to visit. On the first Sunday of June, Stewart and I visited Christ Cathedral Church (under the leadership of Pastors, Dr. Leon Stutzman and his wife Connie). At the time, we did not know the pastors were celebrating their 28th wedding anniversary and were on vacation. As we entered the church, the friendliness of the people was the first thing we noticed. We felt comfortable in the large crowd of strangers. The second thing we noticed was the great sermon delivered by guest speaker, Pastor Dean Lundsford. Pastor Lunsford spoke about the Shunammite woman who took care of the prophet Elisha and who did not have a child. In the bible text, 2 Kings 4:16-17, God tells the Shunammite woman that this time and this season next year, you will be blessed with a child.

> **"The ancestor of every action is a thought."**
> ▪ Ralph Waldo Emerson

It was a sermon which radiated through my spirit and reminded me of my recent experiences. The pastor said, "When God tells you to move you will be blessed or you will have to wait for the next opportunity!" He called it the "Kairos Season". It is a time of divine opportunity and being in the right place at the right time. After the 8.8.8.8.10 dream I became very familiar with God's set time and I realized there are certain periods to respond to a door of opportunity. The words of "seasonal timing" resonated deep within my spirit. I knew I was in the right place at the right time and every word of knowledge was for me to absorb. The pastor said, "God is speaking to someone to make a move in their life and this is the time to make that move." The following Sunday we returned to the church to hear the prophetic teachings of Dr.

Stutzman and we have been there ever since.

In June 2000, I became a Mary Kay Beauty Consultant, under the directorship of Mary Ford. Mary, who was known for her big smile and big heart, inspired me to get the most out of the business. She was a great friend and mentor. In August of 2005, Mary lost her courageous fight with cancer. Her spirit of excellence is still with me today. During her illness, Mary continued working her business while in the hospital. She was dedicated to empowering woman to do their best. She was a real inspiration to me and hundreds of other women!

In August 2000, after almost a five year hiatus, I was ready to return to work. It was a blessing spending the time at home with Tia and the twins. Although I found myself in a different office than my previous position for the City of Dayton, I was blessed to be working within a division with some of the same co-workers, who had moved their because of promotions. It was good to have familiar faces on my return to the daily 8 to 5 job.

## Called to Serve

Christ Cathedral Church has been like a portal to many blessings. During early 2001, I experienced an unusual and detailed dream. In the dream, which took place in a church sanctuary, the pastor told the parishioners to clean something in front of them. I immediately got out of my seat and knelt down to clean the dirty floor. As I looked back, I noticed no one else had left their comfortable seats. They were just content to wipe off their bibles. When I awoke from my dream, I understood there was a job for me to do. A few weeks later, Dr. Stutzman invited church members to get connected and volunteer in the children's ministry. It really did not take much to persuade us to volunteer in children's ministry because our twin daughters, Veronica and Victoria, were benefiting every Sunday in the care of volunteers. In addition to paying tithes, Stewart and I also believed in volunteering and investing our time. Volunteering is a simple way to show gratitude for your blessings. It is the law of reciprocation. As you bless others, others will bless you.

## Friends for A Lifetime

While serving in children's ministry we met Jesse and Veronica Hines. We shared a lot in common including raising young children and they befriended us right away. They treated us more like family than friends and our relationship grew beyond the boundaries of the church. Over the next several years, we ate together, traveled together, played together and prayed together. It was like we were all part of a large extended family enjoying life's adventures together. We thank God for our lasting relationship with the Hines family.

## The Spiritual Journey

In late May of 2001, Stewart attended a local spiritual retreat, the Greater Dayton Emmaus Walk, after being invited by his friend John Stoddard. Prior to the retreat, Stewart and John had been sharing their Christian walk and their desire to build a closer relationship with God. Earlier in 2001, John attended the retreat and was greatly enlightened by the experience. He wanted Stewart to also experience the positive effect of the retreat. I am very grateful to John, because after the retreat, which lasted for several days, Stewart was energized and committed to building a closer relationship with God. The few days that Stewart attended the retreat transformed his life forever.

## A Day for Prayer

On September 11, 2001, the United States suffered almost 3000 deaths due to a terrorist attack. The surprise attack was executed by 19 al-Qaeda terrorists, who hijacked four commercial airliners, intentionally crashing two of the jet planes into the Twin Towers in New York City. The majority of American deaths occurred when the Twin Towers fell to the ground. It was not only physically devastating, but the entire country was psychologically damaged. In the dust of the devastation, God made his presence known as the entire country came together and prayed for the families that had lost someone. Stewart and I were at our jobs in downtown Dayton that day. The downtown streets that were busy with commuters in the morning were completely deserted by noon. It was very eerie, almost like the world had stop turning for a couple hours as we tried to catch our collective breath. Especially at a time like this, we were grateful for God's comforting hands.

**2001 —**
*Girls' first day of kindergarten!*

## Stretching Our Tent

In the last few months of 2001, Stewart and I started to look for our new house. Four females sharing one bathroom was eventually going to be a problem, especially since Veronica and Victoria were getting older. Pretty soon the bathroom door would be closed all the time, leaving Stewart very few options including the gas station restroom down the street. The one bathroom was not the only reason for moving. Our neighborhood sometimes sounded like a "war zone" because of all the gun fire. It was not safe for anyone, but especially young girls and women. After seven years of living here since the start of our marriage, I was ready to look for a bigger house (with more bathrooms) that was located in a safer neighborhood.

Looking for a house is exciting and scary at the same time. It was fun imagining yourself living in the house of your dreams. House hunting is also very confusing because there are so many available at one time to look at. Our friends Jesse and Veronica told us about a house on the market they wanted us to see. It was in their neighborhood and across the street from their house. We liked the house, but thought it was overpriced and mentally knocked it off our list of possible new homes. The following year, we came very close to purchasing a home but changed our minds at the last minute. In May 2002, Stewart and I moved into a four bedroom, two and half bath dream home, a month before Tia graduated from high school. It was the same house that our friends had told us about several months ago. Not only did the house stay on the market for several months, but the price dropped. We thanked God for our amazing blessing.

## Miracle on Liscum Drive

In April of 2003, my girlfriend Louise Plant, after returning from a trip to California to see her sister, was in a horrific life threatening car accident at Liscum Drive and US State Route 35. We have been friends since her son, Christopher was a baby — almost twenty years. We talked almost everyday. It was God's good grace and a miracle that Louise survived the accident. The accident actually involved her SUV flipping over and landing on her head and fracturing her skull. God was with Louise every step of the way, as several "Good Samaritans" lifted her SUV off her head and saved her life. Louise does not have any family in town, so I thank God I was here to pray for her during hospital visits. God answers prayers and there were a lot of people praying for her. Louise was very close to death, so it was a blessing to see a miracle of preservation. You can read more about Louise's personal account of her experience on page 257.

## Good Times

During the hot summer of 2003, we joined the Hines family on a vacation road trip to Virginia Beach. The travel caravan included the Hines family, as well as our children (Tia, Veronica and Victoria, in addition to our nieces Tamara and Taja). The 10 hour drive that took us through the scenic mountains of West Virginia and Virginia was breathtaking. Prior to leaving for the trip, Stewart had sprained his right angle in a freak accident after an eye exam, so driving for long periods of time was a challenge for him. The first couple of days/nights we stayed in a hotel in downtown Norfolk. During the day, we would drive over to Virginia Beach and walk along the shoreline and shop. It was great spending time with our friends, who treated us like family. On the third day, Stewart and I really wanted to find a hotel and stay on the beach. It was at the height of tourist season so every hotel was either outrageously priced or already booked. Through an amazing miracle, our oldest and resourceful daughter Tia was asked by a stranger if she was looking for a place to stay on the beach. That stranger was a nice lady named, Ms. Betty Blalock. She generously offered to let our family stay in her timeshare beach front condo, that was available for one night for free! God is good! We were complete strangers and she trusted us to have full use of her place with no strings attached. The condo, which overlooked the beach and ocean, was fully equipped with a kitchen and nice bedrooms. We made good use of the kitchen and made a spaghetti dinner for our entire travel party. The memory of Ms. Blalock's generosity is still fresh in our spirits. It is a great reminder of God's love and goodness that impacts our daily lives. Every year, Ms. Blalock and our family exchange Christmas cards. God bless Ms. Blalock for her kindness.

On the last day of our great vacation to Virginia Beach, I spent the last few hours shopping for an unique souvenir. I believe souvenirs are special symbolic reminders of the places you have visited while on vacation. Some people like to buy things they collect, like mugs, postcards or figurines. I like lighthouses because they remind me of God and his beacon of light that always leads you out of a storm. As I was browsing through the last shop, I found a five foot tall lamp that was in the shape of a lighthouse. It was beautiful and unusual — a great find for my collection! I was so excited about my lighthouse lamp that I rested the lamp shade on my lap the entire trip back home because I did not want it to get damaged. Whenever I enter into my living room today, and look at my lighthouse lamp, I am reminded of the fabulous experience in Virginia Beach.

## Another Miracle of Preservation

A few days before Easter weekend of 2004, Stewart called his mother but she did not answer. La Verne was a very independent woman, so it was not unusual for her to be out somewhere at the store or running several errands. On Good Friday, a friend of Laverne's, who usually talks to her everyday was concerned when she did not hear from her. The friend notified church members and the pastor called us. We immediately drove over to her house. At first we could not find LaVerne. The television, lights and kitchen stove were on. On the stove there was a pot of beans burning that had been there for some time. The pot of beans were burned to a crisp and the house was filled with a light haze. It was a miracle that the stove did not catch on fire. Stewart finally found his Mom at the bottom of the basement steps. We believe she had fallen while walking down the steps but could not get back up on her feet. She was alive, but very weak and dehydrated from spending two, maybe three days, on her back on the concrete floor without any food, water and medication. It was the grace and preservation of God that kept her alive. After arriving at the hospital, LaVerne's condition was very critical. Stewart and I spent a couple hours praying that God would improve her condition. Laverne's condition did improve and she was moved to a nursing home for rehabilitation to improve her mobility that was affected by the fall. In three months, LaVerne was able to leave the nursing home and go back home. We were happy that God had given us more time together. Over the next five years, LaVerne struggled with health issues and left this life for heaven in September 2009. On the beautiful funeral program Stewart designed, there were words that read, "LaVerne Left A Legacy of Love." That was very true.

Laverne was always good to her family and friends. She also managed to raise two amazing and caring sons. Unlike typical in-laws, we had a good "mother and daughter" relationship for 15 years. I treasure my time I had with LaVerne and miss her very much.

## The Power of God and Prayer

In 2005, our friend John Stoddard was diagnosed with a form Germ Cell cancer called Seminoma. It was the same cancer that Lance Armstrong had. John was in a battle for his life. During grueling sessions of chemotherapy, John relied on God, his loving wife and the support of family and friends for daily strength. Everyday Stewart and I would pray for John's healing. He had a lot of people praying for him. About half way through the difficult chemotherapy sessions, which left him very weak, John told Stewart he could actually feel the many prayers. After several months of treatment, John

> **"Then He spoke a parable to them, that men always ought to pray and not lose heart..."**
> ▪ Luke 18:1 (NKJV)

began to recover and regain his strength. Stewart still recalls the day that John returned to work and shared the news he was cancer free. It was a great day because all our prayers were answered and our dear friend was cured. Prayers always change everything. You can read more about John's personal account of his experience on page 213.

## Promotion and Opportunity

In 2005, almost five years after returning to work, I received a promotion. I left the Building Services division and began working as a Project Telephone Technician in the City of Dayton Police Department. The new position, that involved transcribing audio police reports, was interesting. Sometimes when I typed it was like having the pages of a good book develop right before my eyes. The hours were the most difficult part of the job. I worked second shift, which meant when my family was at home, I was at work. Although I liked the job, it was very isolating because all I did everyday was interact with machines and paper. I did not have direct interaction with the public, but I began to pray for people in the reports concerning their daily struggles. The struggles included domestic abuse, death of love ones, suicide and other life issues. I asked God to put me in a place where I could provide more help for more people. Sometimes you should be careful what you pray for because you never know how God is going to answer you.

In November 2008, my job typing police reports was abolished and I was offered a position of a 911 Emergency Operator. I knew this was a very stressful job and I really wasn't interested. It was a fast paced position that required the operator to talk clearly and I had an accent. Although I was born locally, my accent has been described as "Caribbean". Because of my accent and very fast speech patterns, some people said I was difficult to understand. I did not think I was suited for the position. Surprisingly after a few weeks of training, I eventually became comfortable with the position as a 911 Emergency Operator. Each day I would pray before answering the phones and talking to the public. Although some of the calls were hectic and sometimes involved desperate circumstances, it was a blessing from God for me to be the calming spirit on the other end of the phone. I really enjoyed helping people.

## Loss of Some Special People

In January 2008, our friend Jesse Hines called us with the sad news that Veronica's mother, Maria Sanchez (and two other family members) were tragically killed in a car accident. We had met Veronica's mom several times during family gatherings and always enjoyed her graceful and beautiful spirit. It was a loss that was felt by many. Everyday we prayed that Veronica and her family would find comfort and peace from God at a very difficult time. Our time here is so short and we never know when God will call us to go home. Mrs. Sanchez's life on earth was short, but she left a great "inheritance of grace" and a good testimony of God's love for her family and friends. You can read more about Veronica's experiences and the positive influence of her mom on page 283.

In August 2008, our friend Charles Dannin unexpectedly passed away while at work. He was very special to us because Charles along with his wife Rosemary were responsible for setting up Stewart and I on a blind date 15 years ago. We were also connected forever because of the birth of each of our adorable miracle twins.

At the time I was working as a Project Telephone Technician and typing police reports. I was not at work the day the police report concerning the death of Charles came through. As I returned to work the next day, I received the shocking news of our friend's death. Due to the heavy volume of police reports I was told I would not be able to attend his services. After explaining to my supervisors, what Charles meant to my family, I was able to change my work hours and go to the funeral. You can read more about The Dannin Family on page 239.

## Blessings Abound

Several years ago, I was given the opportunity to drive a Mary Kay pink Cadillac. Mary Ford, who was my Director at the time had earned the car through production sales. When Mary became too ill to drive, she would generously let consultant team members drive her car to seminar events. I recall being afraid and thinking, I can not drive this big car. Once I was sitting on the smooth leather seats

> **"A man's reach should exceed his grasp, or what's heaven for?"**
> . Robert Browning

behind the wheel, I became comfortable and really enjoyed the experience. That amazing short drive down the road in the pink luxury vehicle inspired me to work towards a Mary Kay car of my own. After nine years as a Mary Kay consultant and working hard on team production, I earned the use of a brand new Pontiac G6 car in February 2009! It was a wonderful experience leaving the dealership and driving home in a car that I had worked hard to get. I was thankful to God, my director Shirley Williams, and my team members who helped me to achieve my dream of receiving a Mary Kay car.

## Achieving GOALS

In May 2010, my daughter Veronica was the only student from the Mad River School District to advance to the 2010 Power of the Pen in Wooster, Ohio. Power of the Pen is a writing competition for young writers in seventh and eighth grade. Veronica competed in the regional competition and was rewarded with an invitation to the state finals along with 720 writers from 280 schools in Ohio. She represented her school district well by making it to the final round which included 50 writers.

During their eighth grade year at Mad River Middle School, Veronica and Victoria continued to get good grades while also participating in various school activities including sports, the student newspaper, honor club and talent shows. They also used their leadership skills and helped organized the lesson plans for a bible study group that met after school hours.

After working hard on her studies, my oldest daughter Tia, graduated from Sinclair Community College with two associates, one in Psychology and the other degree in Liberal Arts in June 2010.

Stewart and I are proud of all of our daughters and pray they will continue to pursue all their dreams with excellence.

## A 25 Year Journey

Twenty five years ago my life was a chaotic mess that was twisted out of shape because I was living in an abusive relationship. Like every young woman, I dreamed of having a loving relationship and living happily ever after. When my happiness was tarnished, my life was thrown off course like a small life boat in the middle of an angry ocean. I prayed to God for my life to change. The 8.8.8.8.10 dream was the beginning of change, even if I did not realize it at the time. My husband at the time thought he knew the meaning, but the dream was not meant for him. The vision was designed specifically for me at a specific time in my life. I did not think about the dream everyday or even try to figure out what the combination of numbers were. It was like God planted a seed that needed time to mature. God was preparing me for great things, but my life was filled with clutter. As soon I left my abusive circumstances my world around me began to change. If we stay in situations that are destructive to our well being, then we limit or distort God's beautiful vision for our lives.

We must get rid of the baggage we do not need in our life. A few years ago, I had a dream where I was floating high above the earth in a hot air balloon. The view below featured a picturesque and breathtaking blue ocean. As I gazed through the transparent pieces of the puffy clouds, I could see a lighthouse along the shoreline. When I looked in the opposite direction there was a mountain side filled with castles. It was a beautiful world created by God. As the balloon began to slowly descend back to earth, I saw a small home overloaded with stuff. It was very cluttered. I heard a voice clearly say, "Get rid of the clutter in your life and make room for God."

Dreams are very important for our existence because dreams are the seeds of future success. Whether you dream while you are sleeping or dream while you are awake, it is part of God's plan for us to think big and set goals. If we have faith in God, the size of our universe is only limited by our imagination.

My life 25 years after the dream has been a significant journey. I am married to a loving husband who is a wonderful father to our three daughters. Along the journey, Stewart and I were blessed with some amazing people who were an inspiration in our lives. We are thankful for those enriching relationships that are a reflection of God's love. It is part of God's plan for us to have relationships and share our experiences with each other.

The 8.8.8.8.10 dream was a beautiful divine word from God that showered my life with blessings of abundance. The experience was so powerful it left me humbled and also with many questions. Why did God use numbers and what do the numbers mean? While reading the bible I have noticed that particular numbers are often repeated. The number 40 is repeated multiple times throughout the bible and usually refers to "a period of trials":

- Acts 1:3 — Jesus teaches his disciples for 40 days after the Resurrection

- Moses was in Egypt for 40 years before being exiled

- Moses wandered in the wilderness for 40 years

- Genesis 7:4 — The Great Flood lasted 40 days
  and 40 nights

God in his infinite wisdom communicates with us through language and numbers. God is absolute and so are numbers. When God gave me the numerical puzzle, I did not know what it meant but had a sense in my soul of its importance. As the numbers were released into my life I understood that seemingly randomness was not random but specific patterns of time. After 25 years, and my quest for answers, this is what I have discovered about the numbers in my dream and the perpetual blessings that continue today:

- "8" is defined as a new birth or beginning. Four "8s" indicates a series, so there were four new beginnings.

- The number "10" means completion or divine order. When the last "8" happened and the twins were born, the dream was complete.

- It has been 25 years since the dream. The number 25 represents "forgiveness". Not only do I forgive myself for the mistakes of the past but those who have trespassed against me.

- Stewart and I have been married for 17 wonderful years. The number 17 is defined as "victory". The number 17 has symbolic significance in our life because every milestone has happened on a 17:

  • We met on January 17, 1993

  • Our engagement occurred on September 17, 1993

  • Stewart and I were married on September 17, 1994

  • The book, "DreamQuest - A Journey of Significant Vision" was completed in our 17th year of marriage

## Design the Life You Want

It is my hope that anyone who reads this book finds some inspiration to overcome any obstacles placed in their path. I want everyone to know that there is an amazing hope if you have faith in God and desire to change your perspective. Your situation can change, but you have to make that first step forward to release the abundance that God has for you. While I was in my abusive relationship years ago, everyday was the same until I decided that this is not the life God had designed for me. If you are in a corrosive relationship that is taking away your joy, then you need to trust God and find the courage to move on. It was not easy for me, but after letting go everyday was a little better and clearer. I believe God released the 8.8.8.8.10 dream to me only when I was ready for a new positive beginning in my life. The bible says in Jeremiah 29:11 (NKJV), "For I know the thoughts that I think toward you, says the LORD, thoughts of peace and not of evil, to give you a future and a hope." God has a promise and plan for all of our lives, but we can not let our goals and aspirations be hidden by darkness. Our dreams are illuminated by the hope and love we find in God. I thank God for giving me a vision and the many blessings that have been released in the lives of my family and friends. It has been a significant journey!

A journey with hope can bring peace with every step

**My beautiful family!**

*God has blessed me beyond my imagination!*

# Some of the Amazing People I Met Along The Way

**My** 25 year journey would not have been the same without the wonderful individuals that God put on my path. I do not believe we fell into our relationships together by coincidence or accident. These special individuals were strategically placed by God in my life and the lives of my family. Stewart and I are blessed to have these people as friends.

In the following pages you will meet our seven extraordinary friends who will inspire you to reach for your goals and achieve excellence. They are all great examples of striving for a great abundant life while having the courage and faith in God to overcome obstacles.

**"There is nothing on this earth**

**more to be prized than**

**true friendship. "**

— *Thomas Aquinas*

# Dr. Shirley Clark Stallworth

*Shirley is a woman of excellence and grace.*
*She believes in the absolute goodness of God.*

**BIO**

Dr. Shirley Clark Stallworth was born in Memphis, Tennessee and currently lives in Dayton, Ohio with her husband, Tilus. She has a son who lives in California with 4 children. Dr. Stallworth is a full-time professor at Sinclair Community College and has spent the last 19 years in the Computer Information Systems department. She is a staff pastor at C2 Church under the ministry of Bishop Leon Stutzman. Dr. Stallworth is a member of a small church group, Amazing Grace, which sponsors several outreach programs throughout the year. In addition to serving on various other committees, she also enjoys reading and writing.

### How we know Shirley...

We have attended the same church together for the past several years, where Shirley and I serve as staff pastors. Stewart had the pleasure of photographing her wedding in 2009 (while I assisted). It was wonderful being part of Shirley's special day. We are blessed by her warm spirit and strong sense of confidence.

# A Pursuit of EXCELLENCE
an interview with Dr. Shirley Clark Stallworth

*DQ:* What is the story of how you began your journey towards higher education? How did your parents influence your desire for higher education?

**SS:** I really would like to tell you this whole idea behind education. I was raised in a dysfunctional environment because my mother was an alcoholic. My mother went to the seventh grade and my father to the eighth grade, so education was always paramount in our family. I remembered once when my brother and I were running up and down the hallway in our house, excited that we did not have to go to school and how our father got upset with us. So my father said, "Well, if you feel that way about school, then you never have to go back!" So my brother looked at him and looked at me and said, "What is his problem?" He wanted us to be educated. They always appreciated the value of education.

*DQ:* What was your attitude towards learning and how did it help you?

**SS:** When I was in school I always excelled scholastically because my books were my best friends. I was always getting honors for something. I don't think it was because I was academically on a different plane. It was because I had the steadfastness to continue and study. I studied hard. So the by-product of me studying hard was good grades. I have four degrees.

*DQ:* Were there people early along in your journey that helped you?

**SS:** There was so much in between those degrees because I always had people to help. When I was in high school, I did not do very well in algebra. My teacher took me to the side and asked, "Shirley, did someone tell you that algebra is hard?" I said, "Yeah, my eighth grade teacher!" When I was getting ready to go to high school, we had a program called college preparatory, so I was aligned with that because of my grade point average. The whole time I heard algebra was going to be hard and you need to study. So that is what I had planted in my mind. We always talk about the power of the mind and the battlefield of the mind and I had positioned my mind to think algebra was hard. My high school teacher told me that I could do the algebra and that I was just afraid. She was right. After I embraced what she had said and let go of the fear, I was able to grasp the concepts and then I got A's and B's. It was just overcoming the fear. **She was the first person to really believe in me and we need people to believe in us. She saw something in me that I did not see in myself.**

*DQ:* How did the relationship between you and your brother help in achieving your goals?

**SS:** I was competitive. My brother went to school and received his Associates degree. He has a degree in Psychology and he is also a mediator.

*DQ:* So your quest for higher education was fueled in part by competition with your brother's achievement and your desire for success. Did you have any obstacles getting to College?

**SS:** My education has been a journey. My father was a gambler. He was a bricklayer and in those days it was seasonal work, which means he did not save a lot of money. My father had promised to send me to school. I had targeted Sinclair Community College, because I thought it would be a good place for me and it was affordable. Although because of financial circumstances, we could not come up with the money.

*DQ:*How did you overcome your financial difficulties?

**SS:** I am going to talk about the power of God and how, (if we trust in him), we will reach our manifested destiny. I was devastated because my father could not come up with the money and I did know what to do. I was 17 years old when I graduated from high school and in those days I could not get a job because I was not of legal age. I could not do anything but sit around and twiddle my fingers. I remember I had my head down and was crying so hard. Even though my mother and father never went to church, I always wanted to be in church. I always had a relationship with God. I told God I really wanted to go to school, but we didn't have any money. I had no idea how they got my name (maybe it was the universe), but the phone rang and it was someone from Sinclair Community College. They said we have a co-op opportunity for you and you can go to work four months and to school four months — so, that is how I was able to go to school and get my Associates degree.

*DQ:* Now that you have your Associates degree, how did you take your next step forward and what lead you to continue?

**SS:** Sinclair had just begun an articulation agreement program. If you took certain courses while getting your Associates you could articulate into a 4 year school as a junior. So I had taken advantage of that and articulated into the University of Dayton. **While at UD, I met a gentleman who was in my program that made me fall in love with literature and he also helped me along the way.** In fact, he was on my doctoral committee at the University of Cincinnati. After getting my Associates degree, I got my first technical job at NCR. I worked towards an undergraduate degree at UD, because I knew the industry would not take me seriously. I majored in Education and received my Bachelors degree.

*DQ:* How did your achievements in education contribute to your advancement in your professional career?

**SS:** After getting my degree from the University of Dayton, I got a job at NCR as an Educational Curriculum Development Analyst where I developed courses. After I developed the courses, I would go into the classroom to validate the courses to make sure the students could absorb what was taught. I realized after developing those courses, I would walk pass the classroom and miss teaching. I think God always wanted me to be a teacher. I was promoted to an Educational Analyst and this allowed me to not only develop courses, but also travel around the country to teach. I traveled all over the US teaching the Unix operating system, which at the time was my specialty. In those days they did not know what to do with an African-American woman in a technical field. It was a rare opportunity that I would have a job like that. I did that for eight years and traveled as far away as Hawaii. That was nice but I did not feel I had any kind of life.

*DQ:* For the last eight years, you have seen the country and taught many. What was the next stop on your journey?

**SS:** Prior to getting my Associates degree, I started off at NCR as a clerk. They referred to me as a "pink sheet girl" because I would take the pink sheet off of one paper and put it on another paper. I went through various jobs while working on my associates and undergraduate degrees at NCR. A gentleman named Tony Mann, who once worked in the same department at NCR where I was secretary, became a chairperson at Sinclair Community College. He hired me to work at Sinclair part-time teaching Unix while I still held my job as an Educational Analyst at NCR. While teaching, I heard about an opportunity at Sinclair called "Grow Our Own" program. I did not know what they were growing in this program, but I found out they were growing African-Americans with higher-level degrees. They selected me and paid for my Masters degree. This is not tuition. This is not tuition refund. This is not me paying for it and Sinclair paying me back. This is God! The only stipulation was I had to get my Masters degree in three years and I did! My job depended on it. If I wanted to become a tenured track professor, I had to get my Masters. A Masters degree is thousands of dollars and I did not pay a dime! It was God!

*DQ:* How long did it take to get your Associates degree?

**SS:** It took me seven years to get my associates because I had my son to take care of and also had a job. I knew I could take six credit hours a quarter and get finished. I did that until I got finished, because God has given me the ability to stay focused. When you get an education and apply for a job, they are not going to ask you how long it took to get your degree. They just want to know if you have a degree. I always tell my students, whatever you do, put yourself into it.

*DQ:* Do you think your type of perseverance would be valuable to others in overcoming obstacles?

**SS:** Some might say I'm too old. We are at an enormous part of history where competence out weighs age. Look at the airplane pilot that landed the plane on the Hudson River and saved all the passengers. He was in his 50's. **Don't worry about things that you cannot take care of. Let God take care of it. If it is something for you, then you will get it.**

*DQ:* How did you begin the process of getting your Doctorate degree?

**SS:** While working on my Masters degree I met a lady who embraced me and suggested I get my Doctorate degree at the University of Cincinnati. I had to pass an exam to get entrance. You had to be interviewed by the chairperson of your committee after passing the entrance exam. The chairperson sat there and ask me, "Shirley just tell me why you want to become a doctor." I heard this voice as clear as day say, "Look up!" The voice said, "Read the titles of those books in his office and make sentences out of them." I looked up at the titles and constructed sentences saying why I wanted to become a Doctor. It was God! God strategically puts people in you life. When I was working on my undergraduate degree, the gentlemen at UD told to me to go to Wright State to get my Masters. While at Wright State a lady suggested that I go to UC for my Doctorate. When I arrived at University of Cincinnati, I was instructed by the voice to read those titles. God saw me through.

*DQ: God has been a big part of your success. How has your relationship with God helped with other parts of your life?*

**SS:** I dated Tilus, (my husband), for four years before we got married because I wanted to finish school first. There was so much going on in my life, I really do not know how I got it done except for the help of God. It all seemed like a dream. It's about God's timing for you. My mother was an alcoholic until she was about 89 when she went through detoxification. She is 98 years old now and has been in a nursing home for about eight years. I had decades of sadness, because I kept asking myself when would my Mother stop drinking. You don't think it will ever happen, but God said when it was time. I now have the best relationship with my Mother.

> "I really do not know how I got it done except for the help of God."

*DQ: Do you have any future dreams or aspirations?*

**SS:** I am currently working on an adolescent program called Straight Talk Safe Space. The program, (which was developed by myself and

Tim Tilk), mentors to young men (ages 11 – 18) who do not have a role model at home. In addition I am also developing a workshop for family functioning and working with the African American Mentors program at Sinclair Community College. I also would like to travel.

# John Stoddard

—John (on right) with his good friend Stewart

*In addition to being a great family man,
John has a big heart for God.*

---

### BIO

John loves Jesus... and John's greatest desire is to be a radical disciple of Jesus — one who thinks like Jesus, talks like Jesus and acts like Jesus.

John was born in Phoenix, Arizona into an Air Force family originally from Detroit, Michigan. He lived in several states across the United States, including three years overseas in Japan, until landing in Dayton, Ohio as a young teenager. Today he calls Dayton home where he lives with his wife Sarah who he has been happily married to for 25 years. Together they have raised two sons, Ian and Devin; and a daughter Morgan. Recently John welcomed Elizabeth and her four year-old son Ethan into the Stoddard family when she was married to Ian. John loves being a grandfather and is hopeful to be blessed with many more grandchildren.

John enjoys the great outdoors and loves taking his family camping in the vintage 1974 camper that Sarah and John restored. They love spending time together and serving the Lord together through several ministries at their church; John especially likes the times when he gets to use his graphic design skills to promote church events and programs.

---

### How we know John...

Stewart has worked with John for several years at the City of Dayton. John is regarded as a good friend to Stewart as well as the family. We can always depend upon John for words of advice and prayer. In 2001, John was Stewart's sponsor to The Greater Dayton Walk to Emmaus, a local spiritual retreat. I will always be grateful because that experience made Stewart a better husband and father.

---

# Walking in the SPIRIT
an interview with John Stoddard

*DQ: In 2001, you participated in the The Greater Dayton Walk to Emmaus. What is the Walk to Emmaus and how did it change your life?*

**JS:** A friend of mine invited me to a weekend retreat. I had no idea what it was. It ended up being The Walk to Emmaus. It is a Christian retreat presented by the Methodist Church and is modeled after the Cursillo that was founded in the Catholic Church. I spent 72 hours at the retreat which is actually a short course in Christianity for people who love Jesus and are looking for a way to further develop their relationship with God. It is not for new believers but for people who are ready and willing to expand their faith and get to know God a little more. You are right, it was a life changing experience for me. My experience on the Walk transformed me from just believing in God to knowing God. By this I mean, I knew God in my head and that weekend, through grace, I was able to move God's Love to my heart. I began to not only know God but I could feel God in my heart.

*DQ: I appreciate and remember when you invited Stewart on the retreat. It was a good experience for him. At the time we were going through a transition at a new church.*

**JS:** Well Stephanie, you know God comes into people's life when they least expect it and when He knows they need it. I remember that time very well. Stewart and I were working closely together in the same office at the time and we talked about the Lord often. After my Walk I was so filled with the Holy Spirit I had to share this feeling with my friend, so I invited him to go on the Walk. And God did the rest, and changed Stewarts's life as well.

> **DQ:** *Can you tell me how your life was prior to your relationship with God? How did your spiritual growth begin?*

**JS:** Long story short, I wish that I had come to know the Lord a lot sooner because I was a restless kid who got into a lot of trouble that I shouldn't have. But I know if I didn't have the past that I did, I wouldn't be the person I am today. **So, I think all things happen for the greater purpose of God, because I can use my past and identify with other people's struggles.** I was baptized and raised Catholic and attended mass with my mother, my brother and my sister but Dad did not go with us. After I got married and before I came to the Lord, I was a C&E Christian and attended church only at Christmas and Easter, which were the two most crowded days of church. My wife and I did not attend Mass regularly. I knew Jesus but my life was not filled with the Lord. I did not look for hope in the Lord. I thought I could do this on my own and I was a lone ranger trying to make ends meet. Life didn't change until we started going through some financial hardships. My wife, Sarah, started going back to church to find peace and would take me along (sometimes kicking and fighting). The more I went, the more I was okay with it. We got involved with a small church group which is very similar to what is happening today with home churches. People think the home church is new but actually it is an old practice going back to the 1st century. In our church we established small church groups where three or four couples would meet on a regular basis in each other's homes for bible study and to talk about their own spiritual growth. That is really what excelled my personal spiritual growth because I got to meet other people with similar backgrounds and struggles who were trying to find peace in Christ. I think that really helped me focus on God because from there I read my bible more and more until I went on my Walk to Emmaus. That is when things really changed for me. **Before Emmaus, Jesus was Jesus. At Emmaus, Jesus became my Lord.** The first 40 years of my life I lived without Jesus as Lord and I pray the following 40 are an improvement where I can work for the Lord instead of working against him.

*DQ:* *When were you diagnosed with cancer?*

**JS:** I found out I had cancer back in 2005 and have been in remission for five years now. 2005 really turned out to be a pivotal year of my life. Even though I was a Christian, I was tested way beyond belief and to my amazement it sent me further on my path and trust in God. During Christmas of 2004, I thought I hurt my back while shoveling snow and pushing people's stuck cars out of the snow. By spring, my back did not get any better and that's when the year took it's turn. My oldest son went through a traumatic situation and received a DUI. Sarah, my wife, had a hostile takeover at her place of employment and didn't even know if she would have a job. During this time period, my youngest son graduated from high school and a week later my daughter, who was 16 years-old had to have her second open heart surgery, this time to repair a leaking valve. This all happened the first half of the year and the whole time my back was in pain. During that time, I started walking a lot because of the stress and began losing weight. It felt better when I walked. After my daughter's surgery, my back was so bad that I could no longer lie down because of the pain. That is when I talked to my friend Kurt one morning and told him, I think I am dying and need to see a doctor. Soon after that is when I was diagnosed with cancer. At this time, one of my sons was preparing to go off to college while the other son moved to Florida. I had my CAT scan early one morning and by the time I got home, Kurt, my best friend who happens to be a doctor, called and told me I had cancer and I said, "No, seriously what is going on?" He said, "No, seriously you have cancer," and I did not believe him. My friend finally convinced me that this was not a joke and he needed to see me immediately. That is when I handed the phone to my wife, Sarah, because I zoned out and Kurt explained the cancer to her. Before we left the house we called our good friends John and Marilyn. John is a pastor and my sponsor to Emmaus. We all met in John's office at his church and we prayed. Then we went to Kurt's office and before I knew it I was standing there looking at film that showed a tumor in me shaped like a football and the size of a small loaf of bread. Kurt prayed with us.

*DQ: What was your initial prognosis and how did prayer help you during this time?*

**JS:** They thought I had Lymphoma and that wasn't a very good prognosis for a fifty-year old man. We left the doctor's office and stopped by my brother's place of employment that was close by and my brother prayed with us. Sarah and I talked a lot during that day and later I called my brother, Denny and six of my closest friends to explain to them what was going on and asked them to pray. This may sound odd, but I don't just ask anyone to pray for me because I don't know how they are going to pray. I went to men I knew were men of God and would pray the way I needed for God's will to be done. The next week I had a biopsy to figure out what kind of Lymphoma cancer I had. And each day that followed, my friend, my doctor, would call me and say they don't have a diagnosis and they cannot figure out what type of cancer it is. This went on for six days. That night Kurt called and said they still don't have a diagnosis and they only have one more slice to test. If they cannot determine a diagnosis, I would have to have another biopsy. For a week the men I had called had been praying. Again Kurt called on the seventh night and this time with a confirmed diagnosis. He told me I had a Germ Cell cancer called Seminoma, commonly known as testicular cancer. It was the same cancer that sport's legend Lance Armstrong had. I found it good news when my Oncologist told me that there are two forms of cancer that is curable in men and one of them is Seminoma — a much better diagnosis than Lymphoma! Some folks may be skeptical but I know in my heart it was the collective prayer of these Godly men that changed everything. The diagnosis should have never taken that long, but prayer changes things. My Oncologist consults with the same doctor in Indiana who treated Lance Armstrong, so I received the same medical treatment. Keep in mind Lance was in his twenties when he was treated and I was twice his age. The chemotherapy treatments were grueling and my fifty year old non-athletic body took a hard hit as I became weaker each day with the daily treatments that went on for many weeks. I cannot thank God enough for the best wife a man could ever ask for than my wife Sarah. She took care of me 24/7. **It was her constant companionship and unconditional love that got me through those difficult months. I cannot think of anyone else I would have wanted by my side than my Sarah.**

*DQ: Now that the doctors know how to fight your cancer, how did you mentally handle the process of treatments and getting better?*

**JS:** Sometime after my biopsy, during that week, the reality of not knowing what kind of cancer I had started to set in. I remember asking Sarah if I was going to die. As people found out about my cancer they would say they would pray for me, but I didn't want them to pray for me. In fact, at that point I did not know how to pray for myself, especially after the diagnosis. So I turned to my Bible and read a lot. While reading St. John's Gospel about the Prayer of Jesus before He was arrested, I remember stopping at a particular verse. I kept reading it over and over. **"Father, they [the disciples] are your gift to me. I wish that where I am they also may be with me, that they may see my glory that you gave me, because you loved me before the foundation of the world" --John 17:24.** I read it as if God gave the disciples [us] to Jesus and Jesus' desire was to have them [us] be with Him in Heaven since that is where He was going to be. Because of this I went through a period of time thinking I cannot pray for physical healing because it is contrary to what God wants for me as His disciple — and that I should be dying and that I shouldn't pray to be alive. At that point I wanted to please Jesus and be in Heaven with Him. I really struggled with that and for a short period of time. I remember talking with Sarah and Kurt and other people in my life about it. Then one day while talking to Kurt, he told me about a movie he had seen years ago and then said, "John, this is what I am going to ask you as my friend and it is a quote from the movie, 'are you going to get busy dying or get busy living?'" I remember thinking about that the rest of the day and decided to get busy living. I started praying for myself in a new way and my whole attitude changed just as I was beginning my chemotherapy, which was very grueling. After I chose life, I remember people saying, 'I will pray for you' but I told them don't pray for me because I am going to be fine and I am in the hands of the Lord. I asked them to pray for my wife and children because the burden on them is more than the burden on me. After several months, my chemotherapy was finished and I began to feel better. I slowly regained my strength and went back to work part time for a month before returning to my full time position as a graphic designer.

> **DQ:** *How did the possibility of death and your bout with cancer change your perspective on life?*

**JS:** Cancer will change you and I don't think it's necessarily the cancer that changes you. It's when you come to the realization that you are dying. I remember standing in the parking lot after a breakfast meeting with Kurt and saying, "I need your help because I am dying." Until you go through the experience of knowing, I don't think it can be explained what that moment is like. Anyone reading this who has ever experienced that moment will know what I am talking about. It is when God and the Holy Spirit begins to talk to you. That is the moment your life changes forever. Until you experience an event that is radically life changing you probably will not understand. Whether it is, knowing (like in my case) you are dying and choosing to live or accepting God as your saviour, I can honestly say those two moments overlap in time and space and are one in the same. When you choose to live here on Earth and when you choose to live for Christ with a sincere heart, it is exactly the same. Back in the 1970s there was a popular saying, "today is the first day of the rest of your life". Most people focus on 'today' as their new beginning. I have chosen to look at 'today' much differently because the opposite for me is true. I say every day is the last day of your life! What if today is actually the last day of your life? What is your relationship with God today? Did you think like Jesus, talk like Jesus and act like Jesus? If you believe that today is the last day of your life than you are living your life in the presence for God.

*DQ: What dreams have you fulfilled and what future goals would you like to achieve? What is most important to you and your family?*

**JS:** As a husband and a father we are told to be the spiritual leader of our household and as a member of the body of Christ we become a priest in the brotherhood of all believers. This really puts a man in a precarious position. I remember going to church as a young boy and at the end of Mass the priest would always say, **"Ite missa est", which is Latin for 'go forth, you are sent'.** It refers to when Christ told His disciples to go out into the world to spread the 'Good News'. Since the Mass is no longer in Latin the priest says, "The mass has ended, go in peace to love and serve the world." And if this is what I am created to do 'to spread the Good News of Jesus Christ' and if I cannot take care of my own house first, than how can I take care of things outside my house? My primary goal and desire is to teach my children, especially my sons, about Jesus Christ and how much they are loved by Him. My daughter has Down Syndrome and through her unconditional love she probably has a closer relationship with Jesus than anyone can imagine. Because she is not skewed by worldly things she accepts Jesus for who He is and not who the world says He is. I desire for my sons to live in the world today and love Jesus and not to be ashamed by letting it be known. How can I go out to teach the love of God and the Good News of Jesus Christ without bringing it to my home first? No matter how long it takes, and with my wife's help, my goal is to teach my sons to become men of God; so they will become spiritual leaders in their households — and teach their wives and their children about God's mercy and grace, and to take the Good News out into the world.

*DQ: Are there any particular scriptures or prayers that have helped you on your spiritual walk.*

**JS:** Recently at a church meeting we were talking about prayer. I know a lot of people like you and Stewart write a prayer for your family at the beginning of the year which is a good practice. The question was asked, do you have a family prayer or favourite verse of scripture? I do not really have a family prayer but I have two things that I live by. First is my favourite verse. Before I became a Christian, when I was just starting to go to church and reading the bible, I was taken to court by a co-worker for something I did not do. I remember reading Philippians 2:3 in the bible, which states, "Do nothing out of selfishness or out of vainglory; rather, humble regard others as more important than yourself." I read that passage repeatedly and meditated on the words and it was the first time I had done that with scripture. Usually I would read the Bible to just get through it but that day I discovered I was reading the Bible to change my life. That little verse did change my life in a big way and it was the defining moment that I began seeking God more. I was cleared of the charges brought against me and I asked the judge to forgive

> **"Do nothing out of selfishness or out of vainglory; rather, humble regard others as more important than yourself."**
>
> **Philippians 2:3**

my co-worker as I had done and to let no penalties come onto them, which he granted. And then there is the beginning of a prayer to the Holy Spirit that I focus on also; "Come Holy Spirit, fill the hearts of your faithful and kindle in them the fire of your love. And you shall renew the face of the earth." Through my meditation on this prayer I discovered what the Holy Spirit really means to me. As Christians we always talk about God and we talk about Jesus, but we don't talk much about the Holy Spirit. The world has taken God out of school and has written Him off; and Jesus becomes the one that people can talk about, but there is no talk of the Holy Spirit. Without the Holy Spirit, what we believe as Christians about the resurrection of Christ would not have happen. I realized the meaning of the Holy Spirit one day while reading in the book of John (19: 30) at the end when Christ was dying on the cross; "When Jesus had taken the wine, he said, 'It is finished.' And bowing his head, he handed over the spirit." It dawned on me then; after Jesus died, that THE HOLY SPIRIT that dwelled in Jesus Christ my Lord as a man on the cross is the same Holy Spirit that lives in me today, as well as in all of us who believe JESUS IS LORD!

# Pastor Robert W. Lyons Jr.

*Robert is a modern day "Renaissance Man"*
*filled with faith and hope for the community.*

**BIO**

Pastor Robert W. Lyons Jr. is a graduate of the University of Dayton, B.A. in religious studies. After 11 years with the City of Dayton working in technology, Pastor Lyons, and his wife founded Word of Faith Christian Ministries (Now, The MarketPlace Movement).

Pastor Lyons Jr. has a unique passion to see the will of God manifest in the earth through collective vision of practical and relevant ministry. The MarketPlace Movement was birthed to provide an "Out the Box" experience that will impact all facets of your life.

He shares the call that God has on his life with his lovely and dedicated wife Jamila Lyons.

Pastor Robert Lyons Jr. is the proud parent of three children and he strives to lead their lives and the ministry utilizing the blueprint found in the word of God and the implementation of consistent ministry excellence.

### How we know Robert...

Robert was a co-worker of Stewart's when they both worked in the Public Affairs office at the City of Dayton. Not only have they worked on projects in the workplace, but also on several free-lance projects together. Stewart calls Robert the modern "Renaissance Man", because he is willing to take risks while learning and he is not afraid of any challenge.

# A Quantum Leap of FAITH
an interview with Pastor Robert W. Lyons Jr

*DQ: You started early with success in your life after being a W. S. McIntosh Memorial Leadership Award recipient — what is the W. S. McIntosh Memorial Leadership Award and how did you benefit?*

**RL:** The W. S. McIntosh Memorial Leadership Award is a partnership between the University of Dayton and the City of Dayton. They select one African American student who resides in the city and they give them a four year scholarship to the University of Dayton, as well as, a four-year internship with the City of Dayton. The scholarship is based on merit. They look at your grades but also look at your involvement in the school and the community. It is not bias and you can't just have great grades. Some people may have wonderful grades but they will ask you if you were involved in extracurricular activities. If you weren't involved in anything then your grades should have been good. To be honest I wasn't going to apply for it at all, but at the last minute I told my mom that I was going to apply for it. This is the first time I heard my mother say, "Your faith is a little different". At the time prior to that I had received a lot of packages from a lot of colleges and when I received the information about the W. S. McIntosh program, my mom said, "The University of Dayton is very expensive" and told me I needed to apply to these other schools. I said, "No, I am going to get into University of Dayton and they are going to give me this scholarship." She stated how do you know and I replied, "I just feel it, I am going to get this scholarship." When I arrived to be interviewed, it was interesting, because there were people applying for the same scholarship with earlier appointments who I had gone to high school with. I knew what their ACT/SAT scores were and their scores and grades were much higher than mine. Although I graduated in the top 10 percent of my high school class, all my classmates applying for the scholarship graduated ahead of me but I still knew this was my scholarship. **I went through the interview process and by time I had made it home, they had already called to tell me I had received the scholarship.** That is how I started my working career with the City of Dayton.

> *DQ:* What was your work experience like at the City of Dayton during your internship?

**RL:** During the first year of your internship with the City you do a whirlwind tour and you go to all the City's departments and divisions. You are given the chance to see how the City operates and they schedule you a couple of work days in each area. I was able to see every aspect of the organization. I began my college career as a music major. Normally, the City of Dayton would do their best to place the interns in a department that is related to their major, however I was a music guy and they did not know where to place me. I was finally placed in the City's television office, which was a function of the Department of Public Affairs. They thought since I wrote music, I could compose music for their original programming that aired on television but they could not figure out anything else for me to do. I was moved out of television and into the main office of Public Affairs. William Gillispie, who was Deputy City Manager at the time, knew I was good at computers and ask me have I ever thought about building a website. I knew computers but I had never built a website in my life. I told Mr. Gillispie I would need a couple hours to think about it — he gave me overnight to make a decision. I left City Hall that night and went to a bookstore to pick-up a complete idiot guide to HTML (the code for building websites). The book was over 400 pages, but I read it in one evening. The next morning I accepted the job (of building websites).

*DQ:* How much is W.S. McIntosh Memorial Leadership Award worth?

**RL:** The entire scholarship which included schooling and the internship was worth over $100,000 at the time I attended the University of Dayton.

*DQ:* You appear to be a person who is not afraid of challenges or the opportunity to learn something new — what is another example where you were successful at learning on the fly?

**RL:** When Valerie Lemmie was the City Manager I recall her coming into my office and saying she was going to Africa tomorrow morning and here is my presentation that I would like put on a CD. I stated, "You only want the date on the CD?" She said, "No, I would like an interactive video that viewers can click and go to certain sections of the presentation." **Even though I had never done anything like this before, I told Ms. Lemmie that I could do it.** At the time we did not have the software to do anything like this. I downloaded a 30 day trial version of software and began working immediately on the presentation that was due the next morning. I enlisted the help of John Stoddard, a graphic designer, who worked in Public Affairs in the Reproduction Services area. John and I worked all day and night to meet the deadline. As the custodian left the building, he gave us the alarm code, so we could set the alarm when we were done. We finally finished the presentation and left for home between 3 a.m. and 4 a.m. I went home, changed my clothes and met Ms.

Lemmie at the Dayton International Airport and handed her the finished CD presentation.

**DQ:** *Was there a great emphasis on educational achievement in your family?*

**RL:** My mother, father and oldest sister never finished college and my brother dropped out. My younger sister and I were the only ones to finish college. With them it was always a push to do it. My dad, who was a entrepreneur, told me if I did not go to college for four years, I could go to Sinclair Community College for two years and then work in the family business — **But I was inspired and driven to do more.**

**DQ:** *What challenges did you overcome while completing your degree?*

**RL:** When I went to University of Dayton, I really wanted to be a music major but that was my plan and not God's plan. **Attending the University of Dayton was a God thing.** I turned down a scholarship to go to Hampton, where I was going to major in sound engineering. I also had money from Juliard and some other high end music conservatories but UD was where I was suppose to be. They actually formulated a program for me that was mixed with sound engineering and music composition. It was a God thing. I started off with music composition but once I figured out that I was not going to make any money, I decided to switch majors and study computers. It was still my plan and not God's. The University of Dayton is a catholic school with a very high level of educational standards and here I was changing my major for a third time to Religious Studies. Remember that my scholarship is only for four years.

I am not Catholic and I am changing my major to a religious study in a catholic university in my junior year. Since I changed my major, I was informed by the university that there was no way I would be able to finish a four-year degree in two years, especially since my scholarship would be exhausted in two years. They told me to figure out where I was going to get the money I needed to complete school. For me, just being told I could not do it, was enough motivation for me to get finished in two years. It was challenging but I completed my degree in two years. Being told I can not do something is a motivator for me.

*DQ: Do you consider a challenge something that motivates you?*

**RL:** Sometimes I need someone to tell me I can't do something and if you don't tell me I can't, this has actually been my "Achilles' Heel" because I will take my time. I thrive on challenges. In high school I was selected to a program called Boys State. It is a government mock program and Ohio is one of the biggest participating states. The event which was held at Bowling Green University, involved running a mock political campaign. The highest position you could run for was governor. If you obtain that position, you could attend the national event, Boys Nation, with an opportunity to meet the President of the United States. Out of the 1550 boys in attendance less then 50 were African Americans and I did not want to be there. The gentlemen that had taken me to the program suggested that I run for the governor position, but I was not interested. As the day progressed I realized that a lot of people there did not think I could become governor. This cause me to become interested and challenged, so I ran for the position and made the governorship. In 1996, I had the pleasure of meeting President Clinton in Washington, DC. It was a phenomenal time.

> **DQ:** *Describe what you enjoyed about your job while working for the City of Dayton. How difficult was it to leave your job?*

**RL:** I loved my job. Working for the city was interesting because it gave me my first glimpse into trying to get jobs done with all types of people. I still remember my journal entry from 2003 when I started pastoring. I asked God to let me be able to pastor my church and quit my job. I remember begging God to quit because I can't imagine working for the City of Dayton and being a pastor too. I had no ideal how I would get paid and take care of my family. At that time I had been promoted and was doing quite well with the city. The last project I had implemented was Kronos (an employee time-management system). It was a million dollar plus project and I was the project manager. Even though I was a young man under the age of 30 managing a major project for a major municipality, I remember asking God to let me out of this place but God was very clear and said your work here is not done. God said how can you pastor when you have not effectively ministered to the almost 2500 people who work in the organization that you are in. When they know that you are called, then I will let you out. I realized I had been spiritually silent during most of my time at the City. People knew that this is Robert and that he loved God. They even knew when I started my church but I was spiritually silent. I was more of a pen light then the light on the hill.

> "I remember asking God to let me out of this place — but God was very clear and said your work here is not done."

Once I became that light, then God said, ok you can leave now. **Leaving my job at the City after almost 11 years, was the hardest and the most fulfilling thing that I have ever done in my life.** I remember carrying my box of personal items out of my office, turning off the lights and walking to my car in the garage for the last time — asking God if I had made a mistake. As I held the box in my hands I was crying my eyes out thinking I have messed up. Maybe I should not have done this. I had no idea what I was doing. All I knew was that God had done this.

> **DQ:** *What were some of the obstacles you faced with your ministry after becoming a "full-time" pastor of a church?*

**RL:** We overcame all kinds of obstacle because the risk started immediately. When I worked for the City I received a paycheck every two weeks so when you step out you never know what is going to happen. Even though it was difficult, my wife was there every step of the way. I used my entire retirement that I had accumulated over the last 11 years and put it in my church and to live day to day. I was like a poker player. God this is either going to work or it is not. **I remember standing up in front of my leadership after I left my job and telling them as passionately as I could that the Lord is my Shepherd and I shall not want.** That word "want" means I shall not decrease, shall not lack and I shall not be in need. Right then I understood all of my help came from the Lord and not from them. It is rough knowing that some of these same people that said they had my back are no longer with me today. It was difficult at first, but it was also very fulfilling figuring out how to juggle being a pastor, father and husband. I would have thought that since I was not working full-time for the City that the burden at home would be less.

It was actually easier while working at the City to be a pastor, father and husband, than taking the city out of the equation. I don't believe you can really determine how much something means to someone until your life depends on it. All of a sudden I had to come to terms with all of the areas of my life that were out of balance. I could not spend all night getting the church together and neglect my children because they still needed daddy to talk to them and share things about their day. I also wanted to spend time with my wife, Jamila. We promised each other to never put our children in a position of hating church, because we spent all of our time concentrated on the church and not enough quality time with them. I remember listening to a nationally known minister and his daughter, who is a grown woman, who said to her father, "We did not know you growing up and you were not there". My wife and I have agreed never to do that to our children. We always want to maintain normalcy for our children. It has not been easy. This past Sunday was a prime example. My kids were in a dance competition which was suppose to have happened on Saturday, but the event got switched to Sunday morning. We were in the middle of a big series at the church, and normally I would ask someone else to preach. My wife told me that I can not leave in the middle of a series. I am literally messed up because my babies are dancing and I am trying to figure out how do I get to Columbus Ohio and pastor our church in Dayton Ohio at the same time. We made the decision to split-up. My wife went to Columbus, while I preached my message. I was torn. This was a big decision for us because for many of my peers this would not have been a consideration. The fact that Jamila and I could even have the conversation demonstrated how much I wanted to see my kids dance. It meant a lot to us.

*DQ: How has your relationship with God, family and friends helped you to stay focused on your goals?*

**RL:** Because of my DNA, and enjoying the challenges of life, my relationship with family and friends has helped me not necessarily because they pushed me but often time because they didn't. Other than my wife and a few ancillary people around me, I have not had that go get them group of people. I more have had that, uhmmmm, maybe you shouldn't. Even when we started the church a very prominent member of my family told me, "You do not have any money, you don't have a building, you have no people, this makes no sense. Why would you even do this?" My response to this person was, "Didn't you tell me to have faith in God?" This has been the road that I have been on. Very close friends that started with me just vanished. I think that I have been fueled a lot by a broken heart. **It really has taken my wife and the Lord to keep me focused.** God stays consistent when everyone else is fickle. It is true I did not know what I was getting into. I had no idea.

*DQ: How has the relationship with your wife given you the support you needed?*

**RL:** My wife is my rib and the rib protects every vital organ. It protects the heart, it protects the lung, it protects everything vital and it actually gives structure to the body. Once I understood that she was the rib for me, I understood why she said the things she said. It is because she is trying to protect me and bring structure to the body. It is my divine job to lead our family but Jamila actually ministers to me. The more we walk in that role together, the more we fall in love because she is the one that helps bring clarity to the chaos that I deal with everyday.

*DQ: What do you find rewarding — what gives you purpose?*

**RL:** Saving people's lives. I think for me I am driven by life change. I am driven when I see people apply change in their life. Success is not determined by the number of people we had at church today. I remember during my kick-off service on a Saturday and there were about 500 people that attended at the Convention Center. There were people everywhere. My friend preached which was good and bad at the same time. We had a lot of visitors that day but they never heard me. That was a mistake. On Sunday my attendance had shrunk to 12 people, so I had literally lost 400 plus people overnight. The following Sunday, we got snowed out and the next Sunday we were down to just me and my wife. We had gone from 500 people to just the two of us. I was desensitized to numbers because in my mind we lost 500 people in three weeks. We started asking the question why there were just a few of us sitting around a eight foot table — but I was still inspired. I was inspired when the light bulb went off and one person would say, OH, I GET IT! I am inspired when I can stand now because there are approximately 100 of us and we are continuing to grow. That is my drive. I am also inspired by the small things like waking up in the morning and hearing my kids in worship not because daddy told them to but because they find the joy in wanting to. I am inspired when I can hear my babies reading the word at night without daddy reminding them to. I am inspired when all the lights and television are off and I can hear my little girls praying because in their little way they are asking God to help mommy & daddy. Those are the things that make me proud.

When their mother is sick and oldest child goes to get her siblings to pray for Mommy, I am inspired because now I see the presence of God in their young lives. If I can't see it in my home then I am a hypocrite.

**DQ:** *What advise would you give others pursuing their dreams or aspirations? How do you keep the faith and keep pushing forward?*

**RL:** I think that I would tell others to get the spiritual discipline of solitude first. Solitude is one of the most difficult. I have two spiritual disciplines that absolutely slap me in the face. One is solitude and the other is keeping a journal. Keeping a journal is hard for me because seeing my faults on paper is a lot for me. Solitude is rough for me because of hearing God speak that clearly. As soon as I go into solitude God does not show me people, he starts showing me, myself. It is the mirror of myself immediately. I think that anybody that wants to do this needs to learn how to get into the presence of God consistently because all of your help comes from the Lord. This is true. You have to learn to get in the presence of God consistently and then from there you get accountable. You have to have some mutual accountability with people who are not going to allow you to settle. You have to have a regiment in the presence of God because the study and prayer all will be birthed out of spending quality time with the Lord. He will not let you spend quality time with him and you are not studying your bible. God will not let you spend quality time with him in that crowd in prayer. If people can get that and get accountability, they always will be on the road to greatness. Quality time with God will even tell when you are not called. When you spend quality time with God, he will show you yourself and you will figure it out what you are suppose to do or not do. The hardest thing for me was discovering what I am good at versus what I am called to. Everything that I am good at is not what I am called to. It is like where the scripture says, "To everything there is a season." There are some things that are seasonal that I am good at it but it is not my destiny. I heard one preacher put it like this, "Some things I am doing is because it is my duty, but it is not my identity". I can not allow my duty to identify me. The 11 years I spent at the City working was my duty, but it was not my identity. If I allowed that to identify me I would still be at the City and at this point be out of the word of God because the check was consistent. I can not allow that to identify me. I am now operating in my identity. People see my photographs because I take pictures and say, "Ooh, you should be a photographer!" I am good at it but I am not called to it. There have been times when myself, Stewart, and John were going to put together a media company. We were really going to do it because we were good at it, but not called to it. There was no way God was going to breath on it. It was not because the three of us were not anointed and not good friends. Why would God breath on something he knew would take us away from the plan of God on our lives. If it would have worked it would have been because of our diligence not because of the breath of God.

# Rosemary Dannin

—*Rosemary and her beautiful twins, Sophie and Joseph*
*She has an optimistic view of life and believes*
*we are all connected by love.*

**BIO**

Rosemary was born on November 14, 1959 in Mount Holly, New Jersey. Her father was in the Air Force so her family moved frequently during his military career, until 1969 when he was transferred to Wright Patterson Air Force Base in Dayton, Ohio. Rosemary has three sisters and one brother who passed in 1991. She is a graduate of Stebbins High School and Sinclair Community College. Rosemary currently lives in Dayton, Ohio with her beautiful twins, Joe and Sophie.

### How we know Rosemary...

I have had the great pleasure of knowing about Rosemary since December 1992 (when Rosemary and her husband Charles started the "matchmaker" project of introducing Stewart and I). At the time, we all worked together — Rosemary was a co-worker of Stewart's at Peter Li Education Group and I worked with Charles at the City in Dayton in the Housing Department. We are forever connected through a special friendship and the birth of "our" twins. We love her beautiful and pleasant spirit!

# Living Life As a Magical Journey
an interview with Rosemary Dannin

*DQ: I always enjoy telling people the story of how Stewart and I met. We are forever connected because you and Charles played matchmakers and were instrumental in the birth of our relationship. How did you meet Stewart?*

**RD:** I started working at Peter Li on February 10, 1992. On my first day on the job I was greeted by a beautiful vase of daisies that Stewart Halfacre had left on my desk and I knew that this was a magical place — and that good things were going to happen there.

*DQ: How did you get your name?*

**RD:** The morning I was born there was a big yellow rose that bloomed in the backyard and my father told my mother about it and they decided to name me Rosemary. The rose still exists and is pressed in the family bible at my father's house. That always made me feel very special as a kid. I can remember opening up the bible and looking for that flower.

*DQ: A yellow rose in middle of November in New Jersey is very unusual and divine. What were some of your experiences during your childhood?*

**RD:** My father was in the Air Force, so we moved a lot. When I was three years old, we moved to Illinois for approximately three years. We then moved to Hawaii for three years. Living in Hawaii was a magical experience. I was six when we lived in Hawaii and nine when we left. That experience of being there during that age was just magical. It was like a celebration because everyone celebrated life there. People would sing songs. The public schools weren't great but they taught you a lot about the culture which I thought was really cool. In 1969 we moved to Dayton when my father was transferred to Wright-Patterson Air Force Base. We lived in base housing until 1972 when my father retired from the Air Force. Then we all decided to stay here after my father's retirement. He got a job at NCR and we lived in a house on Eastman Avenue, where my father still lives today. I went to public school where I attended Stebbins High school and graduated in 1977.

**DQ:** *How did you meet Charles and what was your first impression?*

**RD:** In 1981 I was working as a cocktail waitress at the Brown Derby and somebody had mentioned Chi Chi's restaurant by the Dayton Mall was hiring. I remember jobs were really hard to find back then. It was really tough. So I applied and I got a job at Chi Chi's. I remember people coming up and congratulating me and saying wow, you are lucky you got a job at Chi Chi's, because that is where everybody wanted to work. It was the new popular spot. One evening, after working there for a few months, there was a new bartender that was hired and I hadn't seen him yet, so I went in on my day off. I went prancing in, I was all dressed up and ready to go out on the town. I walked in and I saw Charles. He was the new bartender and I remember seeing his profile and the second I looked at him something happened. Something went off in my body, some electrical charge. I thought to myself, ooh he is good looking I think I'll go out with him sometime — just assuming he was available and that he would ask me. I went up to him and I said hello, I am Rosemary and he was very foul. He had a very foul mouth and he said something to me that I don't even want to repeat, but it became a running joke throughout our marriage later on. When he opened his mouth it was like eww, I don't like this guy at all and he really didn't like me. We worked together for six months not liking each other and he was just real ornery, very ornery. He would take liberties that he shouldn't have. We would wear these little peasant blouses and he would pull them back and say, "Oops, are you wearing plain or fancy today?" It was all harmless but I was real offended. I used to have fantasies about throwing drinks in his face and telling him to get lost. During the last month that we worked together, we started talking about other things and really getting into some really deep conversations. We were really looking at each other in a whole different way. I think that he had some walls built because he had been married and his wife left him, therefore he was a little sceptical about dating. Once I started learning more things about him I softened and then he softened. One day we went out to Friday's. We were out for lunch and we looked at each other and he said, **"You know we are really nice people, why can't we find anybody, because I think you are a good person and I am a good person."** We just kind of looked at each other and said, "Well, then why don't we start going out." That's how it started. It took six months of just kind of working through whatever we had to work through to finally see each other. On our first date, we went to Cincinnati and sat on the Serpentine Wall and watched the Ringling Brothers Circus unload the animals. We watched the animals then we went to Union Terminal and had lunch. We spent a really nice day together and from there we were together all the time.

*DQ: How long did you date Charles before getting married?*

**RD:** Our first date was in March. We were engaged in July and then we married in January. It was pretty quick and we were married for 25 1/2 years before Charles passed.

*DQ: When did you and Charles plan to have children?*

**RD:** As soon as we got married I wanted to have children. We tried and we tried, and tried and nothing happened. I started seeing a fertility specialist and they really couldn't figure out what was going on. The specialist was a celebrity fertility doctor at Miami Valley Hospital, who we saw for three years. He had us go through all of these tests and we did the artificial insemination. This specialist finally said he could not help us. When I was working at Peter Li in 1994 I wasn't seeing a fertility specialist any more. I went back to my original doctor who apologized for sending us to a specialist who could not help. My doctor had us start over from scratch to see what was going on. He did an ultrasound and found that I had a rather large fibroid tumor on my uterus but he didn't want to take it out. He was afraid if I had surgery that it would cause scaring on my uterus and make it impossible to conceive. My doctor decided to take one step at a time and preceded with artificial insemination. I remember distinctly an experience that I had prior to starting that whole process. I kept thinking the longer we went on without conceiving the more depressed I got and the more I sort of had it in my mind that I was the unlucky one. That gee, maybe this will never happen for me because I am just unlucky and this is not going to happen. Well, I remember one day saying wait a minute to myself, you know, this could happen for me. I had to change the way

I was thinking. I swear at that moment I felt something wash over me. It was like I cellularly changed and became a woman who was able to conceive.

> **DQ:** *When you changed your thinking this allowed God to be able to move on your behalf — you had to change your way of thinking and be open to what God had planned.*

**RD:** I knew that there was something changed and I knew that I would eventually conceive. I just knew it. There was no question. I didn't know when and it didn't matter, because I just trusted God and I became euphoric! I remember feeling like I was just floating. The first two inseminations didn't take but I didn't get upset. I said, "That's ok," the third one was in July and I just knew that this was the month. On July 28th, 1994, the doctor changed the technique a little bit during a procedure that was done in the office in the afternoon. My doctor told me to go home tonight and take it easy. Well, we went to a concert that night. We ended up driving to Cincinnati to see Crosby Stills & Nash, (one of our favorites), at the Riverbend Music Center. During the song "Deja Vu", a song I used to listen to as a teenager, something happened. I could feel something happening and it is hard to describe, but I just knew and on the drive home I remember feeling so different. I knew that there was something different about me and I remember it was a cool night and we were driving home. I had my window down and there was a cool breeze upon my face and I knew that everything was going to be ok.

*DQ: When did you learn you were pregnant and what was your reaction?*

**RD:** A couple weeks later I started spotting. I think I thought ok, it didn't work this time, but it's going to happen. I am certain things are good. I sort of forgot about it. I figured I would probably have a period and we will try again next month. All of a sudden it was like, wait a minute,

> "Oh my God, I am pregnant after all these years of trying!"

I should probably take a pregnancy test because I am still feeling kind of different. I drove to the drugstore and got a pregnancy test. I followed the instructions and I said, "Oh my God, I am pregnant after all these years of trying!" If ever I had a night when I couldn't fall asleep, I would think about the baby and then eventually it became the babies. I would start thinking about two. I would picture them in my mind and I named them. It was always a boy and a girl and they had several names; Katie and Charlie, Claire and Sam, or Abigail and Alex. There was a series of names and this was years ago before I conceived. I would really visualize actually having the babies and the babies growing up and seeing the two of them play together. I remember having this vision of these two little babies crawling all over me. These were visions that I had. I got the pregnancy test and it was oh my gosh! I am pregnant, we are going to have a baby! Gosh, I wonder when are we going to have that second. I was already thinking about when are we going to have that second child and of course this was around your wedding, which was in September. I got pregnant in July and immediately grew out of that beautiful bridesmaid's dress. I was working out like crazy, trying to keep my weight down and that just was not happening. At the time of your wedding I didn't know that I was having twins but you knew. **You came up to me and said, "Rosemary you are going to have twins."** You told me this before I knew, because I had not had my ultrasound yet. I did not get an ultrasound until a couple weeks after your wedding. I remember telling you to replace me in the wedding and you said, "This was not an option , we will just have to get new dresses."

*DQ: I was really glad that this happened, because I did not want everyone wearing the same dresses. Although Stewart had picked out the dresses, I wanted my sister Karen, who was my Maid of Honor, to wear something special and different from the other bridesmaids. This was perfect — I was happy you became pregnant. Karen wore the dress that Stewart had picked and the bridesmaids rented something else from a bridal store. Everyone was very gracious and we all worked together.*

*DQ: Prior to getting pregnant, were you considering adoption?*

**RD:** Yes, we were on the adoption list for Catholic Social Services. We had been on that list for two years before. I had the pleasure of calling them and saying, I am pregnant. I remember she was so happy for us. The lady at Catholic Social Services said, "We will go ahead and keep everything on file and you can call us after the birth and let us know." I was able to make that call to her right before Easter and I told her that we came home with our twins, Sophie and Joe and she said, "This is the best Easter gift!" It was just so cool! Charles and I both knew that we wanted to be parents. It didn't matter how these children were going to come to us, whether it was through adoption or birth, we just knew that we were put here on this earth to be parents. We both wanted the same thing. It was 12 years after we were married. They were born April 5, 1995. Sophie

Dannin was born at 1:27 and Joe Dannin was born at 1:28 by Cesarean and it was really quick.

*DQ: When you had your ultrasound did you know that you were having a boy and girl?*

**RD:** Yes, we found out that Joe was a boy during one of the early ultrasounds. On Valentine's Day 1995 was when we finally found out that Sophie was a girl. We got the name Joseph because it was always a favorite name of mine. I knew after I got pregnant that if it was a boy Joseph would be his name. Charles chose the name for Sophia, we talked about it and he had picked out some other names that I didn't like. His choices of Rebecca and Esther were not working for me at all. Charles suggested the name of Sophia, a name on his side of the family, which I liked. Therefore, we chose Sophia and we have called her Sophie from day one.

*DQ: How long were you able to carry your twins?*

**RD:** I can remember, I had just turned 35 years of age after I conceived and this automatically put me in the high risk pregnancy category. The concern was going into early labor. I would talk to the babies and I told them that they could not come out until after the daffodils bloomed. We went 38 weeks and they waited on the daffodils. That was our goal. Sophie weighed 6 lbs. 7 ounces and Joseph weighed 6 lbs. 10 ounces. They were nice and big and fully cooked!

*DQ: How did the birth of Joseph and Sophie change your world and the world around you?*

**RD:** Oh my goodness, the moment that I was able to see them... I was able to see Joseph first because Sophie was having a little trouble breathing. They wrapped Joseph up (like a little burrito) and brought him to me. That first moment that I looked at him I thought how can anybody not believe in God. I didn't do this. This wasn't me. It completely changed me. My whole world changed the moment I was able to meet them face to face. **It was like seeing the face of God and it was awesome!** I think that at that moment, I really understood how it feels to live in gratitude.

*DQ: How old are the twins and what are they like?*

**RD:** The twins are now 16 years of age and they are very creative and unique. They are old souls and they have always been very mature children but especially since they have lost their dad. **They are just incredible and amazing.**

*DQ: How helpful and how involved was Charles with the children?*

**RD:** He was great! Charles was there from the day that I took the pregnancy test. He was working out in the backyard when I had said honey come here and I showed him the test. He said, "Oh my gosh, we are going to have a baby!" Charles immediately began thinking about all the things that he had to do. He was in that mode of what do I have to do to get ready. At the time, we were renovating the house which was almost complete. Charles spent the next nine months wrapping it up. He was there from the first moment. He was next to me when they were born. He stayed home with me for two weeks to help after they were born. He made sure that I got enough sleep. After we would eat around 5:30 p.m.

— 6:00 p.m., I would go to bed and Charles took the second shift. I was able to get several hours of sleep and he would go to bed between 11:00 p.m. and midnight. Then I would get up and do that shift, because they ate every three hours. Charles made sure that I got plenty of rest, which was wonderful. He was just hands on with changing diapers, feeding and doing whatever needed to be done. When they were just a couple of weeks old he said, "Why don't you go out and take a drive and do something." He told me he would give the kids their bath. This was the first time he was giving them a bath. When my best friend came over to the house, she didn't have to jump in and help him. She thought it was so lovely that he was giving the newborns a bath and wasn't afraid. He was very considerate of me and my time and made sure I was cared for. I remember checking out of the hospital and one of the nurses asked me if I had any help and I replied, "My husband will be there." She just looked at me like, ohh you poor thing. I got kind of mad, because I knew that he was fully capable and would be fine. He was a real trooper. I told the kids after he died that you had more of a dad in these 13 years than a lot of kids have in a lifetime, because he was so involved in their lives.

**DQ:** *How has your family supported you and the twins since the death of Charles?*

**RD:** My family has been a lifeline for us. They are all incredibly supportive. We now have a family tradition with my extended family and we all get together every Sunday at LaRosa's Pizzeria in Beavercreek. We all gather together and we catch up with one another and it is something that we all love to do. This involves my dad, my two sisters (and their husbands), all who are here in the Dayton area. It is really a wonderful tradition.

*DQ:* How has your life been since the death of your husband?

**RD:** God is good. When he died I really thought that I was going to disappear, because my life was so wrapped up in his. I thought my God, without him, who am I. **I thought I was going to just disappear — and what has happened is that I have emerged.** What it has taught me is that I still feel that LOVE. It taught me that love is an universal love and it is the same love that connects me to you and connects you to Stewart. Love connects all of us together. That is the one thing that I really learned after he died. I was so full of that love and that helped me to heal. It has been a lot of emotional work. It was important to me that I do that emotional work and not side step it and try to work around it. I really just wanted to just hit it head on. I have the love of my family and they have been very supportive of me. I have great friends and they have all been here for me, Joseph and Sophie, to help us through this. It has been a rough couple of years but now I am selling the house. It is time to let this go. The kids and I have been working to get everything ready. We are painting and fixing up the front yard. The plan is to move to the Oakwood area. This is where they will complete their high school education because private schooling is currently too expensive.

*DQ:* Are you interested in another relationship?

**RD:** Last summer I was on Facebook and I noticed one of my friends from high school had posted some pictures from a high school reunion. It was the 35th reunion of the class of 1975 which was held last summer. I clicked on it and I was looking at pictures when I saw this boy that I used to like back in high school. He was at the reunion and I said ohh my gosh this is

Jeff Smith. I noticed that he was one of this guy's Facebook friends. The last time I had seen him was in 1983, right after I had gotten married when I ran into him at the Spaghetti Warehouse. I sent him a request on Facebook. He accepted and we just exchanged written messages. I asked Jeff how he had been and told him that I had lost my husband, but life was good. I noticed one day that Jeff made a comment on one of my photos and I could tell by his profile that he was single and he knew I was single. He was looking at my pictures and I was on his Facebook page looking at his pictures. He looked amazing. He made a little comment on one of my pictures and it was a very nice comment and very complimentary. I didn't respond to that but thinking about it, I probably should have acknowledged something. One evening I was on Facebook and my chat was opened and we were both online at the same time which rarely happens, because usually I have that feature off so that people can't tell. I started chatting with him. "Hey how are you?" He replied, "How are you?" I wrote, "You are really, really cute!" Jeff responded, "You are really, really cute too and your children are adorable!" Therefore, I knew that he had been looking at my pictures and it melted my heart when he commented on my children. Then he asked for my phone number and I gave it to him. I wrote, "I do not give my number to just anybody, so treat it with care." Jeff called a couple weeks later. We started going out and it was amazing, because I knew... **I had sent out a prayer that I knew that there was somebody here for me — I knew it!** I knew that I wasn't going to be alone for the rest of my life and that there was this person out there for me. I didn't know where, who, or what. I thought maybe I would have to leave Dayton, because I dated more then a few guys. I actually started going out about six months after Charles died, just casually having dinner. I had a few relationships and they just weren't compatible. I wasn't making good decisions because I think I was just lonely. So, I had some bad experiences, but I could just tell that this person was right around the corner. I could feel him, he was somebody that I actually kissed when I was 15 and he was 17 back in high school. We started going out and we have so much in common. We have an incredible amount of compatibility. We like to eat the same foods and we cook well together. He reads the same books and we are both into fitness and nutrition. He is amazing. We are both interested in architecture. Jeff is very mechanical and so am I. There are so many things that we have in common, but there are enough things about us that are different too. It is still a very new relationship, but my gosh it is fabulous!

*DQ: Describe the circumstances surrounding Charles's death.*

**RD:** He was working and in his work car. They knew Charles had made it to his first two inspections, because his tags were there. He did not make it to his third inspection which he was on his way to. It was around 10 a.m. and he wasn't feeling well. It was early. He had pulled over and actually put his seat back and was listening to a book on tape. He was taking a rest, because he wasn't feeling good. He basically fell asleep and he died in his sleep. It was very peaceful. There was no violent clutching, there was nothing. I think that I have this sense that it was just peaceful. They didn't find him until 8:00 p.m. that night. Nobody knew where he was and one of the inspectors said to check Veteran's Parkway because that is where he would take his breaks. I talked to somebody recently who said, it was very peaceful when they found him. Everybody was looking for him. The police were out looking for him and my sisters were looking for him. They said that everybody ended up there at the same time and found him. **His**

co-workers said it was very peaceful, so that gives me comfort knowing that he was at peace. I believe everything happens in God's timing. I never felt that I was a victim. If anything I knew that this was a necessary part of our lives. Where do we go from here? What is next on this journey?

*DQ: How did you find your current job?*

**RD:** Charles died August of 2008. In January 2008 I started working full time at Mazer and I was no longer a part-time employee. It was a big day going back to work full-time. I had been blessed for many years to work part-time while the kids were little. On December 30, 2008 the company closed down and I lost my job but I knew that everything was going to be ok. I wasn't worried about it , but it was a shock. I remember thinking now what am I going to do. I knew that something was going to happen. I let everybody know that I was out of a job and I had a lot of people looking out for me. I got a lead for a job at the Foodbank and this was the first resume that I had sent out. I didn't really hear anything for a long time and then one day I got a phone call from the woman who was doing the interview. She happened to be a classmate of mine from Stebbins High School. (I told Jeff that Stebbins High School is the center of the universe, because a lot of good things have happened there). I really thought the position had already been filled, but it turns out they could not find the right person, so I was asked to come in for an interview. I went into the interview and everything clicked. So here is one of my classmate from Stebbins who is interviewing me and the CEO of the food bank, who is also a Stebbins graduate interviewing me. We just all clicked. They offered me the job two hours later. My title is Resource Development Associate. I help with fund raising, marketing and food sourcing. The incredible part of that story is that Charles had driven across the Washington Street bridge before he turned onto Veteran Parkway where he died. The Foodbank sits right on that corner. That was one of the last things that he saw before he died and that is where I ended up working.

*DQ: What are you looking forward to in the future?*

**RD:** I am looking forward to moving into a new place. I am getting a new boss because the CEO is retiring from the Foodbank. The kids will be going to a new school. Joe is looking at attending Sinclair Community College and Wright State University. He wants to attend art school. Sophie will be attending some private art school but she is unsure of where. She is also thinking about Architecture and possibly enrolling in The University of Cincinnati in an Architectural Program. I have a good feeling about my relationship with Jeff. We have talked about our needs. Neither one of us have a need or desire to be married. We did that and I have my children. He has two adult daughters so there is no need for a legal marriage. I told him that my next union is going to be a spiritual union and not a legal union. That is where we are. I am open to opportunity.

# Louise Hargrove-Plant

*As a woman of courage and strength, Louise has put
her faith in God to overcome many obstacles.*

**BIO**

Louise Hargrove-Plant was born September 7, 1950 in Dayton, Ohio. Her parents, Joseph and Gladys Hargrove were from Alabama, near Tuskegee and moved to Dayton, Ohio in the late 1940's in search of a better life and opportunities. Louise graduated from Nettie Lee Roth High School, Dayton, Ohio. After high school, she continued her education and earned a Bachelor of Science Degree from Central State University, Wilberforce, Ohio, in Business Administration. While pursuing her Master of Business Administration degree she attended University of Cincinnati and the University of Dayton. Louise worked in several professions before retiring on disability, as a teacher, from the Dayton Board of Education.

### How we know Louise...

I first met Louise almost 19 years ago when her son Christopher was a baby — and we have been friends ever since. When Louise was going through her traumatic accident, I was there to offer support and prayer at the hospital. I was glad to help especially since Louise has no family here in town. Her courage, faith and will to survive is an inspiration to me and my family.

# The Invincible FAITH to Survive
an interview with Louise Hargrove-Plant

*DQ: How important was education and what role did your parents play in achieving your goals?*

**LP:** Extremely important. I am the youngest of four children. My parents placed strong emphasis on getting an education. They were familiar with the legacy of Booker T. Washington and George Washington Carver, mentors and honored trail blazers from their vicinity. My parents always instilled in us to get an education, because knowledge is something that can not be taken away from you.

The North was supposed to be the land of opportunity. This turned out to be a good move for them. They were blessed, to buy several properties and had what was considered a comfortable life. They had a much better life here than what they had in Alabama. They were able to help send us to college. All of my siblings have had respectful jobs. My elder brother, Henry was a Sheriff, my other brother, Pheodis was in management for General Motors and my sister, Martha was a high school counselor and attained a Doctorate in Education. I was employed at Dayton Power and Light as a computer analyst. Later I was honored to return to my Alma Mater Central State University, as a computer analyst and an Administrator. I finally retired from the Dayton Board of Education as a teacher.

*DQ: How did you find out you were pregnant with your son, Christopher?*

**LP:** Christopher is a miracle baby. I had problems with fibroid tumors in my twenties. Doctors told me that I could not have children because of the tumors. The thought of never having a child was not on my mind. Several doctors suggested that I should have a hysterectomy which would get rid of the discomforts associated with the tumors and since I would not be having any children, it seemed to be a good solution.

As my condition worsened and my stomach felt weighted, I decided to have surgery. When I arrived at my doctor's office to schedule the surgery, I was told I could not have the surgery. Why, what do you mean? **To my surprise, they told me I was three months pregnant.** This was the beginning of my miracle baby, Christopher Phillip Starks.

*DQ: How was Christopher relationship with his father?*

**LP:** They had a wonderful father and son relationship. Christopher's dad was a supportive person and he loved his son dearly. They spent hours during the traditional father and son activities, such as football, fishing, playing video games and just plain talking together.

*DQ: When did Christopher's father die?*

**LP:** Christopher was 12 years old when his father died suddenly from a massive heart attack, on February 23, 2003, two months prior to my car accident.

*DQ: How did you help Christopher deal with the death of his father?*

**LP:** I decided we should spend Easter with my sister in Oakland, California to get away and give Christopher a break from dealing with the sudden passing of his dad. We had an excellent time there.

*DQ: There was a point in your life when you wanted a closer relationship with God — how did your spiritual growth change your life?*

**LP:** I always had a solid religious background. After moving here from Alabama my parents immediately united with Shiloh Missionary Baptist Church. They were active members in their church until their deaths. They served in many capacities. My father as a Trustee, Deacon and Treasurer. My mother served dutifully as a Deaconess, Sunday School Teacher, Missionary Circle President, President of the Mothers' Board and General Sunday School Superintendent. Because of my parents active roles in the church, I had no choice but to be active also.

For over forty years Shiloh Baptist Church was the foundation and base for my spiritual growth and development. I was baptized at Shiloh on the first Sunday in September, 1959, by the late Rev. W.C. Thomas Sr. In 1992, I began promoting Gospel concerts and founded Glory to God Productions. My paths in the gospel arena intertwined with several national gospel artists whose faith were mainly Pentecostal. I eventually managed a national gospel recording choir, namely, Keith Dobbins and the Resurrection Mass choir out of Columbus, Ohio. In a pentecostal dominant industry, the question was posed whether or not I was saved because I did not speak in tongues. I knew I was saved, but because I witnessed the speaking of tongues so frequently, I prayed to share the experience that they had. I felt it was something different and I truly wanted to share in the experience.

I have a dear friend, Minister Irene Revelle-Hawkins, who lives in Cincinnati, Ohio and who was also a member of the gospel choir which I managed. Minister Revelle-Hawkins assisted me with my quest to have that Pentecostal experience. She introduced me to a lovely lady named Mother Rene Robinson. Every Wednesday evening, after work I would drive to Cincinnati to meet with Minister Revelle-Hawkins at Mother Robinson's home to pray and study the bible — years ago it was called "to tarry" or "pray and wait for the presence of the Holy Spirit." I wanted that experience.

In the year 1998, I  joined Jesus Church in Dayton, Ohio, under the leadership of Bishop George Rubin Scott, which was Pentecostal based. I finally had that wonderful experience. One Sunday afternoon, after church, sitting in my car praising the Lord, I started speaking in an unknown language. I didn't know the words that I spoke, but I  was able to interpret every one of them.  I couldn't wait to share my excitement with my friends in Cincinnati. The bible says that if you seek the Lord you will find him.

*DQ:  What events in your life happen prior to your car accident?*

**LP:** I was changing physically and spiritually. I was losing weight by choice and growing spiritually.  Many people thought I was sick because I was losing weight so rapidly. Every Sunday, the Bishop would call me out and would say young lady come here and raise your hand. He would then begin to say, **"You are not going to die!"** I was thinking, I know that I am not going to die. I am losing weight on my own and I am not sick. Every Sunday he would do this, so much, I even became embarrassed.

Sometimes I held my head down hoping he wouldn't see me and that he would call on someone else. He continued this Sunday after Sunday for approximately three months. I would ask myself, why is he saying this? I know I am not going to die and there is nothing wrong with me. I am not sick. I do not have cancer or diabetes. I am doing this because I want to improve my body, my health and my appearance. Both my parents had diabetes and I promised myself, I was not going to go through what they went through. It did not make sense to me then, but the Bishop's words, "You are not going to die", was one thing that gave me hope throughout my accident. Those words were God's preparation for things to come.

Prior to the car accident, Jesus Church relocated and my son and I united with Rockhill Baptist Church, under the leadership of Rev. Doctor Lavon Mann. In the Bible there is a man named Jonathan, the son of King Saul. Jonathan became David's best friend. David was the predecessor to the throne, Jonathan always had David's back. Rev. Mann is my spiritual adviser and my Jonathan. I can truly say, he has been there through my trials and tribulations, the passing of Christopher's father, my car accident and every trauma since. It was in God's plan for me to unite with Rockhill church.

**DQ:** *Describe what happen on the day of your car accident?*

**LP:** Christopher and I had returned from California. Before returning to work on Monday morning I wanted to get my hair done, so I called my hairdresser for an appointment. She said even though it was crowded, if I could arrive before 3:00 p.m., she could do my hair. I got in my SUV and headed towards downtown. When I arrived at the intersection of Liscum and Route 35, the light was red but soon changed to green. I barely entered the intersection when a lady in a red car, ran the red light and broad sided my SUV which flipped over. It was a sunny day and I had my window down. The SUV rolled over several times. The force caused the shoulder strap to break and I was ejected from the truck; my head hit the pavement and my SUV landed on top of me. The next thing that I remembered was a police officer asking me who should they contact in case of an emergency and I told them that they needed to get my son out of daycare and that was it, I passed out.

*DQ: What do you remember after you arrived at the hospital? How did your faith help keep you alive?*

**LP:** I remember waking up in Miami Valley Hospital with a lot of people around me. The doctors were talking to me and telling me that the neurosurgeon there could not do anything for me. They recommended that I see a doctor at the University of Cincinnati Medical Center in Cincinnati, Ohio. The only problem was I could not be air lifted because of the severe damage to my head and I had a 50/50 chance of making it there in an ambulance. I remember Christopher standing on my left hand side asking, **"When is she going to be normal?"**

There were several people there from my job, church and close friends in my room. They were asked to leave because my blood pressure rose.

Everything they told me at the hospital, indicated that I was going to die. I could hear what the doctors said, but I did not receive it in my spirit. In my mind I heard Bishop Scott's prophesy from several months prior, "You are not going to die!" I remember writing Christopher a note, since I was instructed not to talk. The note read, **"I love you and I am going to be OK, this is only temporary."** Christopher still has that note today.

I truly believed that my medical problems were temporary because of what the Bishop told me. That was one thing that kept me going. There were also other prophesies that had not come to pass at that time, so I knew that was not my time to go.

I am told, that while, I was in intensive care Pastor Mann came and prayed for me. One time he prayed and waved his hand over my body. Rev. Mann said, when he got to the hospital and gave his name he was ushered straight to my room. **Upon entering he notice that my head was to the west and my feet were to the east. That is the way the decease are laid to rest.** That day while driving to the hospital and praying for my healing and recovery God directed him to wave his hands over my body. He later told my family that I was going to be alright. I believe that the spirit of the Lord was there. Afterward, family and friends revealed that they looked at my face and saw it mending and healing in front of them. To this day I do not have a scar on my face from the accident. Upon my arrival to the hospital the left side of my face looked like raw hamburger. I did not have any treatments to my face not even a bandage. I believe it was because the medical staff was so concerned about my other life threatening injuries. I thank God for his healing power!

*DQ:* When you decided to take Christopher on vacation to visit your sister in Oakland, California, I remember talking to you on the phone and hearing a voice clearly say — ask Louise for her sister's number. I did not do it, because I did not want to disturb you while you were on vacation. After you returned from your vacation I received a phone call (while I was at work) from Christopher's daycare, that you had been in a very bad car accident. This was my girls' daycare also, and the administrator there remembered that you and I were friends — so she called to see if I knew your sister's phone number. I should have listened to the voice — now I knew why I needed the phone number. I prayed and asked God for direction. Thank God, Christopher had your sister's number. You were in ICU and the doctors needed a family member to make some immediate medical decisions — so I called your sister, Martha, in California and told her she needed to get here as soon as possible.

*DQ:* How bad was your condition and what was your prognosis?

**LP:** Oh my condition was bad. I had an aneurysm in the back of my head. **The accident physically left me with a laundry list of problems.** My skull was severely fractured and there was not one square inch that was not cracked. I had a broken jaw, broken collar bone, broken ribs, broken shoulder blade and a broken elbow, my neck was broken in three places. The muscles in my eyes were damaged and my right eye was crossed toward the center of my face. The muscles were so damaged that the only way to fix it was to cosmetically center my eye where it would appear as though I was looking straight forward. My left eyelid was damaged to the point it would not close. Because my left eye was drying out, they thought I was going to lose it. I had three surgeries for eye alignments and sewing on new eyelids. I had paralysis on the side of my face. At first, I was paranoid about how I looked, but I quickly got over it. When I look at myself in the mirror now it is a reminder of where I have been and what

I have gone through. I also had a lot of broken teeth and they are still being fixed today. After the accident I could not go to the dentist because they would have had to numb the back of my jaw area — and if they had performed that procedure I would had died. So, how were they going to fix my teeth with a broken jaw — what kind of medicine or incentive were they going to give me to fix my mouth? There was none.

While in the hospital in Cincinnati, just prior to my release, the aneurysm ruptured. I thank God for the nurse who found me unconscious, because I might not be here today. Again, I heard Bishop Scott prophesy, **"You are not going to die."** Again, upon his arrival, Pastor Mann was ushered straight to my room after giving his name. He prayed and meditated with me. After surgery for the aneurysm I was able to have other surgeries and dental procedures. God is good! What was meant to be the demise of me was the beginning of a new life.

> *DQ: God was definitely there with you during your ordeal. When I got a chance to talk to the police officer at the scene of the accident, he told me something that you did not realize at the time. There were "Three Good Samaritans" who stopped and lifted your SUV off your body, I thank God for putting them there at that specific moment to help save your life.*

**LP:** There were so many good Samaritans who came to my rescue besides the nurse in Cincinnati. I was able to get the names of the men who lifted the SUV off of me from the police report. I was later able to meet with them personally and thank all of them at an appreciation dinner. Before the police or paramedics arrived at the accident scene, I was not breathing. A large blood clot had blocked my air passage. A young man name James Craft, from New Carlisle, was at the traffic light in his truck with his brother. They got out and James removed the clot and performed CPR on me. There were a lot of protestors saying he was liable for a lawsuit, but, he perform necessary life saving procedures despite the protests. Bishop Scott's prophesy, "You are not going to die" was being fulfilled.

At that time, I was teaching Special Education students. This was my first time with Special Education and I had grown to have a special love for my students. Later, I was informed by James' mother that he was a former Special Education student, who had very low self esteem. I pray James will never ever have low self esteem again.

> **DQ:** *How has this experience of surviving the accident changed your life?*

**LP:** The car accident changed my life in so many ways. I have surmountable faith and trust in God's word. However, the aneurysm was not the end of my medical battles at the hospital. I developed a swallowing problem. All liquids that I drank went into my lungs and not down my throat. I survived the accident and an aneurysm and now was asphyxiation going to be my demise? The medical team agreed that a G-tube inserted in my stomach was the solution. I would then have to rely on tube feeding for my nourishment and fluids. I prayed to God because I did not want to have a G-tube. I took him at his word and believed that he would answer my prayers. I even called my sister and several of my close friends to let them know that I was trusting

> "If you have faith as a mustard seed, you will say to this mountain, 'Move from here to there,' and it will move; and nothing will be impossible for you."
>
> Matthew 17:20
>
> (NKJV)

in God to answer my prayers and not let me have a G-tube. "If you have faith as a mustard seed, you will say to this mountain, 'Move from here to there,' and it will move; and nothing will be impossible for you." Matthew 17:20 (NKJV).

The next day the doctors reviewed the x-rays while I was swallowing and they could not detect a problem. Hallelujah! I had faith and nothing shall be impossible. As of today eight years later, I still do not have a swallowing problem or a G-tube.

This experience has changed my life in so many ways that I feel there is a calling on my life to tell my story. I do not see myself as a pastor or minister, but more as a motivational speaker and a disciple. I want to tell people what I have been through so they can be encouraged to go through life's obstacles with God's help. It has been told to me prophetically that I would have a prison ministry, and I would be an encouragement to broken and battered women. The calling to tell my story has been on the "back burner" since the accident. I had never felt that the accident had closure. I finally can see God's purpose, reason and I can now feel closure.

Recently, I dealt with Breast Cancer which compelled me to tell my story of all the things I have overcome in the last eight years. I have only survived through my faith and the power of God; a near death accident and cancer. I thank God, that my pathology report shows that I am cancer free! I could be comfortable without any cancer treatments but I decided to take preventive measures because of my son, Christopher. It is well with my soul. I want Christopher to get to the point where he can totally rely on the Lord. I pray everyday for him to get a closer relationship with God — then I will be comfortable with my transition to another life.

Everyone at some point is going to be challenged in their life. It doesn't matter how good of a person you have been. You are still going to go through trials and tribulations in which God will be the only solution. That is a part of life. It is just like being in school where you always have to take and pass a test to get to the next level.

After you get over one obstacle you may receive a breather, but it is just a matter of time before you go through something else. I believe it is how you go through your tests. I pray that God will make me a fast learner because I do not want to repeat any lessons. In school if you don't learn the lesson you have to keep practicing, do remedial classes or repeat the entire task. I do not want to go through any remedial classes in order to learn my lessons.

> **DQ:** How are you dealing with a recent diagnosis of cancer? What was the extent of your Breast Cancer and how have you handled the treatments?

**LP:** I was recently diagnosis with Breast Cancer. In December 2010, I found a lump in my breast and it was hard to the touch and I ignored it. In January 2011 it was still there, so I then went to the doctor and had a mammogram, which indicated Breast Cancer. A biopsy came back positive and the cancer was determined to be in stage one. It was two and a half centimeters long, but the good news was it had not spread to the lymph nodes. If it had spread to the lymph nodes a mastectomy would have been necessary.

The cancerous lump had crystallized in one location making it easy to be removed. The surgeons were able to go in and take it out. This procedure was done on my sister's birthday.

I gave permission for the surgeon to check my lymph nodes and to remove the lymph nodes if they were cancerous. There were no indication of cancer cells in the lymph nodes. After surgery, I was informed that women in my age range, usually within a 10 year period experience a reappearance of cancer in other parts of the body. As a preventive measure, I am having mini chemotherapy treatments that consists of four sessions that will kill any cancer cell throughout the entire body.

There are many downsides to this treatment, such as you would lose your hair, sleep deprivation, fatigued, other times you may become overly energetic. Periodically, I wonder if the treatments were worth the anguish. Then, I think about my "Miracle Baby" and the answer is "Yes". I will truly say, I am not coping well with the chemo treatments. After I have the last chemotherapy session, I am scheduled to begin six to seven weeks of radiation treatments  to make sure there are no remaining cancer cells.  In the meantime I will, "Wait on the LORD; Be of good courage, and He shall strengthen your heart; Wait, I say, on the LORD!". Psalm 27:14 (NKJV)

# LeDon Maddox

*— LeDon with his lovely wife Vicki*

*As man of God, LeDon has a rock solid determination to succeed and live a full life.*

### BIO

LeDon was born in Camp Hill Alabama, near Tuskegee. His mother and father moved to Hamilton Ohio where they lived for approximately six months. LeDon's family also lived in Cleveland before permanently settling down in Dayton Ohio. He has a brother (who is deceased) and a sister. LeDon is also the proud father of two daughters, two sons, (one who is deceased) and a step-daughter. He is the owner of a local clothing store and has been married to his lovely and caring wife, Vicki, for 15 years. LeDon spends a lot of his time committed to helping people.

### How we know LeDon...

I was a co-worker of LeDon's at the City of Dayton. When I was pregnant with the girls, I would visit LeDon while at my doctor appointments in December 1995. Even though LeDon was in bad physical condition after a car accident, he was always upbeat and had a great attitude. Visitors always left LeDon's hospital room inspired by his spirit and zest for life. LeDon's determination to overcome any obstacle is a great inspiration to my family and anybody fortunate enough to meet him.

# A Joyful Determination & Spirit of Gratitude

an interview with LeDon Maddox

*DQ:* In November 1995, you were working for the City of Dayton as a Housing Inspector. During Thanksgiving weekend you were injured in a terrible accident involving a collision between your friend's car and a bus. What do you remember about that day and the severity of your accident?

**LM:** I don't remember the exact time, I try not to think about it. I try to forget the past and push pass this. I had the tools that they gave me such as walkers, and special spoons that attached to my hand — a lot of handicap type equipment. I was totally paralyzed, a quadriplegic as they called it. **As soon as I was able to walk I began tossing those items out real fast. I didn't want to be reminded of them.** I just push them back and I did not want to think about it. I am beyond this and as a result of this, a lot of things have been blocked from my memory.

*DQ:* I remember going to the hospital to see you and you were determined to walk and get out of the hospital. I would go to the hospital to visit you because you were so full of energy and had an incredible positive attitude.

**LM:** I had a crazy determination to walk again. When they put me in a wheelchair, I was able to move one foot, my right foot. This is what kept me out of the nursing home. I would paddle with this one foot. In the mornings I would go to physical therapy and look at all these guys who were stroke victims. One guy had been shot in the head and the bullet went out the back of his head. There were guys in there with issues including various illnesses to stabbings. **I nicknamed that place the "junkyard for people"**. Soon I was able to put myself in the wheelchair and I would paddle myself into physical therapy and I would say, "Come on now, ya'll don't got no business sitting around being sad now. Come on now, pick it up, pick it up!" They nicknamed me Smiley. They'd say, "Here come old Smiley!" I was thinking about how sad these people were and it dawned on me that I was the worse one of all of them. These people were better off then I was. They could move their hands and so they were way ahead of me. I was feeling sad for them. I did not have time to think about myself.

*DQ: My father went to visited you and he was so impressed with your positive attitude.*

**LM:** I look back at that stuff and I realize that it was a mind set. I was in rehab for approximately three months. I was taken from Good Samaritan to Miami Valley Hospital for Rehab.

*DQ: How did you encourage other patients and how did that assist in your recovery?*

**LM:** It was good having the wives, sons and daughters of the patients I shared time with at the hospital and rehab say that I encouraged their loved ones. It made me feel good. I could have easily sat there and felt sorry for myself and been wheelchair bound for the rest of my life, but my faith in God helped my recovery.

*DQ: What was your relationship with God like during rehab?*

**LM:** Every morning I would wake up and thank God. I would look at the sun and see the daylight. It didn't matter if it was raining, cloudy or whatever, because I was happy to be alive. I would thank God everyday and say, "I don't know what your plans are for me, but I am glad you allowed me to be here." I was thinking that it was a blessing that he allowed me to wake up. I was thinking I may never recover from this, but as long as you are with me, I don't have anything to worry about. I used to joke with a lot of people that I developed a personal relationship with the Lord because I could not do anything. I could not get up and move around. Therefore, I would lay there and talk to the Lord all the time which helped me develop a special relationship with him. I became like a child. When a child is a baby, he or she just sticks up under you all the time. As soon as that child gains more mobility he or she begins to get away from you. The child starts stepping out and then he or she runs back. During my recovery, I went back to being more like a child, but the more steps I took the more that I started to lose that strong relationship with God because more things started to occupy my time. I enjoyed the time I had with God and I hate that I lost that private relationship, but the recovery part was good.

> *DQ: You still have that personal relationship, but sometimes our daily chores take us away from our private time with God — you just need to make time for prayer and meditation.*

> *DQ: God had his time with you and now your life is a testimony. How are you helping others? What have you shared with others about your experience?*

**LM:** I do look at it as helping people. I have helped so many people since my accident and have ministered to them. I have been open to a lot of ministering. One of my favorite saying is "I put my hands in the Lords hand and I begged him that whatever you do, don't you turn my hands a loose". I held on to the Lords hand so tight that I left my fingerprint in his. I was that adamant about God never letting me go.

*DQ: How did your strong and stubborn determination get you through parts of rehab that you did not agree with?*

**LM:** While I was at rehab it was recommended that I go talk to someone to instill some positive attitude. I would not go because I felt that I did not need to. I didn't want to go and just open myself up to just anybody and say, "I am so mad, I am so depressed and these things are so bad." I don't think like that, so why should I share those thoughts with a psychiatrist. I don't need this. They would say, "LeDon, you need to go," and I would avoid it. About the third time, I went to the class and the first thing the man said was I don't believe in the Lord but I do believe in a higher power. Don't believe in the Lord? I spent about 15 or 20 minutes in the session, but I soon wheeled myself out of there because I could not deal with that spirit of depression. This was my first & last time that I attended that class. I believe you will become whatever you embrace, so if you embrace depression, you will become depressed. I embraced happiness, so I was happy. I knew I was not going back to the class and go backwards on my recovery.

> "I embraced happiness, so I was happy."

**DQ:** *At the time of your accident, Vicki Holman was your fiance. How did Vicki help you with your recovery?*

**LM:** My daughter was taking care of me when Vicki moved me into her house. This allowed them to work in shifts. My daughter assisted me until Vicki got off work. Then my daughter would be able to rest and Vicki took over. This routine continued until Vicki and I got married. Once we were married Vicki was able to take family medical leave to care for me full time daily. Vicki was and still is a wonderful wife. As I continued to recover and get stronger, Vicki was able to go back to work. I did not want to become a handicap and depend on others.

**DQ:** *How did your mental attitude and faith in God help with your improving physical condition?*

**LM:** I continue to grow stronger and regain my strength. You have to have crazy faith to believe that you are going to get better when you have experienced something traumatic. I am amazed at how far God has brought me because people had written me off. The surgeons and doctors would not give me any hope about my chances of walking again. They would not give me any answers. Did I have a 5% or 10% chance? I wanted to hear something. Finally one of the doctors said, "We are not God" and you have to accept that." This is the only time I heard a doctor ever say anything like that because usually they have an ego. That statement "We are not God," was really helpful because I knew who I believed in and where my strength came from. I began to think I am not a bad person, so why did this happen to me? The Lord replied, "LeDon, I know that you weren't a bad person, but you were not growing and just like Job, (in the bible), I had to take you down to bring you up higher. I am higher than before, maybe not the physically, but definitely mentally.

*DQ:* What injuries did the driver of the vehicle you were in sustain?

**LM:** The driver suffered a bruise on his head. He told me later that during the accident I actually put out my arm and saved him from other injuries. I have no memory of this, but he said I saved his life. I know my concern would have been for him and not myself.

*DQ:* What is currently keeping you busy in your daily life — what is important to you?

**LM:** My activities include helping people. That is very important to me. I own Wendel's clothing store and I am training the employees and Vicki how to run the business. I plan to leave behind a legacy. I own several rental properties and I have never raised the rent. The properties are totally insulated and all have new windows in addition to a new roof. Most of the bathrooms are fitted with space heaters in case the heat is off. I really want to make life better for people if I can. My favorite phrase is **"The strongest part of any building is the foundation"**. Nothing can stand without the foundation. If you think about it symbolically the Lord puts everything in his hand and he is the foundation. The foundation says put everything on top of me and I will support it. The foundation of a house is the least thing you will see. In this world, there are too many "roof top people" who want to be seen. They are not a foundation and do not support anything. I don't think of myself as a big shot, but as a foundation, because nothing can survive or live without the foundation.

**DQ:** *What are your goals and future aspirations?*

**LM:** I realize that sometimes I am doing too much. The more you do, the more that is expected of you and you are sometimes taken for granted. While you are helping people, you do not want to handicap them. I enjoy working in the church where we provide meals for the hungry. We also sell dinners for different organizations in the church to help raise money. During the summer we have been teaching lessons to 60 to 70 kids from the community in a bible class. My prayer and hope is to have a kitchen that feeds the hungry three meals a day. Those who can pay can give a small donation, while others pay nothing. I am also looking forward to adding Wendel's clothing stores in the Columbus and Indianapolis areas. My employees are currently being trained to maintain any new stores that may open in the future. I have a real partnership with my employees. I would like to think of LeDon Maddox as a servant of the Lord that can help people. I could easily take the money from the business and buy a lavish vehicle, but my goal is to help others.

# Veronica Sanchez Hines

*Veronica is dedicated to helping people in need.
She truly believes in sharing the love of God
with everyone she meets.*

> ### BIO
>
> Veronica was born in Kingsville Texas and raised in Pasadena. She graduated from Sam Rayburn High School and is the oldest of three girls. Veronica has been happily married to her husband Jesse for 19 years. They have two children and three dogs. She has been employed in the airline industry for more than 20 years and enjoys her job. Veronica enjoys attending church, motorcycle riding and making good memories with family and friends. She is living life the way she wants to be remembered.

### How we know Veronica...

Veronica has been a family friend since 2001, when Stu and I met Veronica and her husband (Jesse) at church. We volunteered together in the Children's Ministry. We quickly found we had a lot in common, including raising our young children. Veronica and Jesse are generous people with big hearts. They have always treated us like family and are always there to pray for us and gives us encouragement.

# An Inheritance of GRACE
an interview with Veronica Sanchez Hines

*DQ: How did you meet your husband Jesse and when did you get married?*

**VH:** I was working for Continental Air Lines and became good friends with a co-worker, Diana Hines, who was also a Christian. In 1990, Diana introduced me to her little brother Jesse who was in town visiting. Jesse and I had a lot in common because both our childhood experiences caused us to become responsible at a very young age. We also were Christians and loved the Lord. Jesse grew up Baptist and I had a Pentecostal background. My parents always said I had to marry someone that had the same beliefs. In 1992 we married and made our home together in Dayton, Ohio. There have been a lot of ups and downs but it has been a great marriage.

*DQ: How did your father's life change after becoming a minister? What was your church life like growing up?*

**VH:** When I was a little girl before my dad was a minister, he smoked and drank. He preaches the word now and is an ordained minster. My dad always says I gave up three things when I gave my life to the Lord — drinking coffee, drinking beer and smoking. We were always in church. As my sisters and I got older, our parents had us at church four nights a week — whenever the church doors were opened. Our parents encouraged us to have a strong prayer life and close relationship with God.

*DQ:* At what age did you realize how important it is to have a strong prayer life and relationship with God.

**VH:** I was about 14 years of age during the time my father had gone blind from a surgery. He had a degenerative type of disease that affected his eyesight. During an eye surgery to prevent my dad from going totally blind, there were some complications. Something went wrong and he actually died during the surgery. When the doctor brought him back to life, blood had rushed into his eye causing him to lose vision in one eye. Sometimes the Lord has us going down paths and we don't know why we are going through life's difficulties. At an early age, (and the oldest of three daughters), I had some mature responsibilities. Because my father was losing his vision and my mother did not drive, I was driving at the young age of 11 in addition to writing checks. When our father went blind, I believed it increased our faith to another level.

*DQ:* How important is your relationship with family and friends?

**VH:** I have always said you can not choose the family you are born into. My parents taught us to appreciate what we have in this world, especially friends and family. If a friend or family member was in trouble or needed help, we were expected to help them. It was nothing for our parents to let a school friend stay over if they were having problems with their parents. **My parents set an example of accommodation and I wanted to become that person for my children. I feel like I have.** It was important to my parents not to have any strangers in our lives. If someone needed help, they were always very trusting and invited them into our home. It was not uncommon, even if we were living in a small two bedroom apartment, for my parents to take in a family in need. I remember sleeping in the living room, while a family of four or five would sleep in our bedroom. I have learned to treat friends as family because good friends will always be there for each other.

*DQ: When did your mother die and when was the last time you spoke with her ?*

**VH:** On January 8, 2008, my mother, aunt and uncle died in a car accident. They were traveling from Pasadena, Texas to Mexico to see their mother (my grandmother) who was sick. To this day, people say, "I don't know how you deal with the tragic lost of your Mom". Our family is very tight knit and we take care of each other. Some people may find this strange, but one of my sisters lives with me and it is not because of financial reasons. I lived at home until I was married. That is how our parents raised us. It is part of the Mexican culture and it is not uncommon. I lived at home until I was 22 years of age, got married then moved away. You stay at home until you get married or go off to school. There was never a question about us moving out when we reached 18. We were always close and we took care of each other and loved each other. People knew that about us and I never had a problem hugging and kissing my parents in public like some people do. I would always tell my parents that I loved them when I hung up the phone or visited their home. **We always had a routine and we would never say "Good Bye" but always say, "Until next time".** The day my mother was suppose to go to Mexico, she did not feel well and the trip was delayed for a day. That was a beautiful thing and a blessing because I got to talked to my mother before the accident.

*DQ: What were the circumstances of you mother, aunt and uncle's death?*

**VH:** My mom, uncle and aunt were still an hour away from Mexico traveling on a two lane Texas highway when the accident occurred. I never went to the accident scene and we did not find out about the accident until two hours later. With help from my husband, we estimated that the accident happened about 10:45 a.m. The police were able to identify my mom because they found her credit card. We still do not know exactly what happened. They had just filled up with gas and they were in my uncle's mini van. My uncle's wife was restless that day and wanted my uncle to take the bus instead of driving the van. She told him, she did not feel right about him driving, but they went anyway. Unfortunately they encountered a semi-truck that morning and we figured they all died instantly and did not suffer. Sometimes I wonder if they suffered because the van was full of fuel when it was engulfed in flames. How long was my mother alive? **I know these are tricks of the enemy and I truly believe that they did not suffer and God was merciful.** I have seen the pictures and have never shared them with anyone except my husband. It was a very tragic scene. The van was so badly burned that we had to tell the state troopers how many people were inside the vehicle and what their genders were. They could not make out the bodies.

*DQ: I remember how pleasant and graceful your mother was. What memories do you have of your mother? How have those memories helped you in dealing with your grief?*

**VH:** Thank God that I had time with my mother before she died. My plans were to raise my children in the Midwest in Ohio where there are four seasons. I really had no plans of moving back to Texas, but God knew. For the next few years, I had a wonderful relationship with my mother and she was able to enjoy her grandchildren. The Lord knows and he gives us the right to make decisions and we have free will. Many people have asked me how do you still do it — God took your family away. I let them know that we have a free will to do what we want in this world, so I am not mad at God. I am upset and feel short changed that my mother is no longer here physically, although she is still with me in spirit. She is here now and she knew how I felt at the beginning and about the things she would miss with her grandchildren — like seeing them graduate and get married. Her grandchildren were her pride and joy. My mother always said, "I can't wait until you get married and have children, because you can love a grandchild even more than your own child." It is a different level of love and for me this was like an honor to give her grandchildren. My mother had a great relationship with her grandchildren and it just brought out the little girl in her. I loved to see my mother spoil my daughters.

It has only been a few years ago, they were young, but they still have the beautiful memories of my mother. That is great and the Lord is still working with me. This past Mother's Day was a different day for me, but it was not as hard as the first one. It was a really good day. I feel especially close to my mother when I am in church, because that is where she always wanted to be and that is where we were on Mother's Day. When my mom was in church she would sing as loud as she could and out of tune, but it did not matter because she was praising the Lord. After my mother passed, I would sing songs at church and it would bring tears to my eyes, because I knew my mother was there in spirit singing with me. I know it makes her happy that her grandchildren are in church giving gratitude to God. Recently I just had a conversation with my children. I told them that we are never going to tell you what to do in life, but we pray that you will finish high school and go to college. I pray that we continue to do a good job as parents and for you to walk with the Lord and have a close relationship with God. This is what my parents passed down to me. It is an inheritance. When my sisters and I were young, my mother never asked us to be doctors, lawyers, scientists or anything like that. She only wanted us to serve the Lord. My mother always wanted her family to know the Lord. During the funeral I learned my mother had been taking her youngest sister to church with her, where they had joined a women's group. This was beautiful because they did not always have a good relationship but she never gave up on her sister. I also shared how my parents worked hard to raised us as Christians. We were teenagers, sometimes, especially on a Friday or Saturday night, we would rather be somewhere else rather than at church but it built a foundation for my adult life. I learned that from seeing my parents and how it is so important for me to have my children in church to see me praise God. I want to set the example that it is satisfying to raise your hand and surrender everything to the Lord.

*DQ: Your father is a passionate evangelist and travels to Mexico often. Do you worry about his safety?*

**VH:** Even though my father has lost his sight, he still travels to Mexico to preach the gospel because he strongly believes everyone should get a chance to know the Lord. My father was born in the United States but had to get a Mexican citizenship to preach. You have to be a Mexican citizen just to preach the word on a street corner or conduct a church service. I do worry about his safety and every time he gets on a plane, I pray to God for his safe return home. There is a lot of unrest in parts of Mexico and they still kill Christians. Despite the dangers and his visual impairments, my father believes the most important thing is to share the power of God and change lives. I wonder sometimes how can a blind man have so much faith, but my father knows the Lord will provide. He has faith in God. I love my father, but it was a little difficult at first to accept that he got remarried after my mother's death. I did not want my father to be depressed and alone. If that is what my father needed was companionship, then I thank Jesus that he found someone.

**DQ:** *What are your future goals and aspirations? What do you consider to be important over the next 10 years?*

**VH:** We are praying we can get our children through college. My husband, Jesse, has developed a program for the public schools (junior high) called Ties 4 Champions. It is a club that meets before and after school for young men focusing on leadership and creating champions. It teaches them how to present themselves and reach for their goals to achieve the best in life. He does all of this for free because the program really is an outpouring of Christ's love and his desire to help people. This is Jesse's project but he has ask me to be involved. We really want what is best for these young men, because there has been a lost generation of young men. We have beautiful daughters who will marry and have families someday, so we want them to have great young man

> "I am not sure where the journey is taking us, but we are open to whatever the Lord has planned for us."

that are responsible and have many goals for the future. The program is blessed and growing. For the first time, Jesse has spoken with the young men at the high school inspiring them to become champions and leaders. Hopefully Jesse and I can go on and touch more people in the world with God's love. I am not sure where the journey is taking us, but we are open to whatever the Lord has planned for us.

# *Seleana's*
# SWEET
# DREAM

### a short story by
## *Veronica Halfacre*

*Something about the author...*

**BIO**

Veronica was born in 1996 just two minutes before her twin sister Victoria. She is actually the middle child because she has an older sister, Tia, who will be 27 this year.

In addition to being a Honor Student, Veronica is involved in Student Senate, church and many other extracurricular activities.

One of Veronica's passion is reading and writing. In 2010, she was selected to represent the Mad River School District in the "Power of the Pen" state writing competition in Wooster, Ohio. Veronica was rewarded with her creative writing skills when she advanced to the final round.

In addition to writing short fiction, Veronica also enjoys painting and drawing.

Veronica attends Stebbins High School and will be sophomore this upcoming school year.

# *Seleana's Sweet* DREAM

## a short by Veronica Halfacre

I closed my front door as quietly as possible. I crept up the stairs as I stealthily avoided the creaky spots. I counted each step and grabbed a hold of the doorknob. Before I walked into my room I decided to congratulate myself with a victory dance. Bad idea.

"Seleana Maria Anderson!" My mom yelled sternly.

"Um, hey mom. What's going on?" I turned around mid-cabbage patch, to find my mom directly in front of me with her arms folded across her chest.

"This is the third time your teacher has called about you sleeping in class! This is completely unacceptable! Tonight you are going to bed at 8:30!"

"That's like five hours earlier than usual!" I whined.

"I'm not having this discussion with you. Go to bed early or you'll be grounded."

That night I ate my dinner as slow as humanly

possible.

"SLUUURRRP!" I ate my spaghetti one noodle at a time to delay my dreaded bedtime.

"Luna, you're acting like a four-year old." Sighed my dad. His tired eyes frowned at me.

My dad and my grandma were the only ones who called me by my nickname. Before Gram passed away she would tell me stories of how I would never sleep at night as a baby. She nicknamed me Luna, for the Spanish word moon. If the moon was up then so was I.

"I know we're asking a lot from you to actually go to sleep," he started sarcastically. "but we're just asking you to try." My dad always had a knack for playing good cop.

"Daddy, you know I can't go to sleep at night." I protested.

"That's why I bought you this." He handed me a box with a picture of a woman smiling in her sleep.

"Oh great. You're gonna drug me." I said dryly. I looked at the box disapprovingly.

"It's not a drug Luna. It's tea that should help you fall asleep."

"Fine, but I won't like it."

"Fine, don't like it, you insomniac." He said jokingly. He pushed away from the table lazily and shuffled to his room.

"I am not an insomniac!" I huffed resentfully. "I just don't like sleeping at night. And my teacher Sister Margaret she just doesn't like me. I have an A+ in her class. I don't know why the old bag is trippin'."

After I realized I was talking to myself I poured a cup of the "Sleeping Motion Potion". Yum. It actually wasn't too bad. It kinda tasted like peppermint, but I didn't feel a thing. I got into bed and said my prayers. I read a book. In fact I finished it. I did a couple push-ups... nada. Finally, I made myself lay still.

"Rock a-bye baby on the tree top," I felt insane singing myself to sleep. "When you're asleep the crazy will stop."

"No it won't." Chuckled an unfamiliar voice. I sprang out of my bed three feet into the air.

"Who are you?!" I screamed.

"Juan Alveraz at your service." A bright smile flashed at me from across the dark room.

"You better get out of here! DADDY!" I screamed even louder. Instead of my voice echoing back to me, the walls absorbed the sound.

"They can't hear you querida. You're dreaming." He spoke with an annoyingly cute accent. His calm Spanish/Southern voice was hard to be angry at.

"You seriously need to get out!" I reached for the drawer on my dresser where I kept my cell phone. I tugged at my drawer with shaky hands. To my surprise the dresser evaporated like a cloud.

"I told you, this is a dream." He flipped on the light. In front of me stood a boy. Um-young man. I had to look up to see his eyes, and I'm pretty tall.

"Who did you say you were again?" I asked even more confused than ever.

"Juan. Sorry about that first introduction. I was very-"

"Corny?" I said finishing his sentence.

"Ha. You could say that." His caramel colored cheeks

turned pink in embarrassment.

"So I'm in a dream?"

"Yes ma'am."

"Do you show up in girl's bedrooms often?"

His face turned pink again.

"Actually you found me. That song you sang must've opened a portal. Usually all that song brings me are sleeping babies. But it looks like I got lucky tonight."

"Juan, you seem like a really nice guy but you sound insane! And I mean that in the nicest way possible." I said sarcastically.

"I know this all seems strange to you. It was strange to me at first too-"

"Whoa. What do you mean it was strange to you at first? Is this... not dream? Who are you really? What are you?" I asked cautiously.

Juan sighed deeply. "Why are you so dramatic? Just sit down and let me finish what I'm saying." He motioned for me to sit on my bed. I carefully patted my bed to make sure it wouldn't vanish like my dresser.

"You opened a portal to the dream realm. Where I'm

trapped. The only way I can get out is if I help you."

"But, I don't need help."

"Yes you do."

"No. I don't"

"Trust me, you do."

"I think I would know if I needed help."

"Then why else would I be here?"

"I don't know! You tell me!" I shouted.

"I'm here because you need help!" He shouted back.

"Of course! Crazy dream boy thinks *I need help.* Wha-what are you doing?"

Juan reached over and pushed a strand of hair from my face. "What's your name?"

Now I was blushing. "My name is," I paused. "Luna." For some reason I felt compelled to give him my nickname. The name I never shared with anyone. Not even some of my family.

"Luna. Moon. That's pretty. It fits you." He looked out the window at the full moon.

We sat in silence for a moment.

"Will you help me Luna?" He looked at me with pleading eyes.

"Yes, I will." I looked up to smile at him, but he was gone. I sat up in silence replaying what happened in my mind.

"RIIINNG!" The sound of my alarm clock woke me up. I sat up in my bed and touched my face where he had brushed away my hair. I don't think Beyonce could've said it any better. Beautiful nightmare indeed.

## Juan

Hook. Line. And Sinker. I played that girl like a fiddle. If I were there any longer I could've got her to marry me. Unfortunately, I don't get to choose when I come and go. I just get this weird sensation and poof. I'm gone. I don't mean any disrespect. She was pretty and all, but that's not why I was there.

Two weeks ago I was playing in the championship game. Five seconds left on the clock and the game was tied. I ran the ball down the court and just as I'm about to dunk on these fools, some punk pushes me down. Hard. So hard that right now I'm in a coma.

When I woke up I wasn't in my hospital bed. I was in this dark, vacant, cloudy room. A book dropped in front of me listing very specific rules to the Dream Realm.

I'd rather not elaborate on them, but rule 325 states that any romantic relationship between the Dreamer and a Realm Person is completely forbidden. Any disobedience to these rules will result in the Realm Person disappearing forever. So even though that Luna girl is unbelievably hot, it wouldn't work out anyway. If I weren't in a coma I'd totally pursue that.

More importantly rule 745 said plain and simple, I only had one more day before I could never return to the real world. Every once in a while I end up in my hospital room where I see my mom holding the hand of my limp body and crying as she prays. My mom needs me. I'm all she has. That's why I need Luna.

The next day, I think. It's hard to tell time in the Realm. Luna finally sang the tune that brought me to her the first time.

"It's about time!" I said appearing in front of her. I

looked down at my watch. Two more hours until poof, GAME OVER.

"OMG!" Luna gasped completely surprised.

"Don't act so shocked." I sat down on the desk in front of her noticing that we weren't in her bedroom. "You should be happy to see me beautiful, so we can help you with that problem of yours." I tapped her nose with my finger.

"Oh no. I fell asleep in class again! My mom is gonna murder me!" She covered her face with her hands.

"Is this your problem Luna? Is your mother abusive?" I asked in my poorly attempted Dr. Phil impersonation.

"No! I have to get out of here! I have to wake up!" She said tripping over her words.

"You can't! We're running out of time." I said urgently, reminding myself to focus on the fact that I was about to vanish from all eternity.

"Time for what?" She began to pinch her arm and I could feel myself shifting.

"Stop that!" I grabbed her hand.

"If you don't help me I'll never be able to leave this place. I'm in a coma right now at the Oakwood Hospital.

My mom is lying next to my bed and I can't leave her like this. I need you." Tears stung my eyes. I no longer felt the need to lead her on. I can't explain the feelings that suddenly took over me. I grabbed her hand and held it in mine.

"Please." I said with a weak voice that scared even me.

I looked at Luna. Her eyes were watery.

"I'm sorry. I don't know how to help you." She gave me hug and looked me in the eyes. I could tell she wanted to help.

I'm not sure why I did this, but I kissed her. The instant our lips touched I could feel myself shifting again. This time I was gone too fast to avoid it. The last thing I saw was Luna's tear stained face.

### Seleana

He kissed me. I opened my eyes and I was back in my classroom. He was gone, and I was sure he wasn't coming back.

"Glad you could join us again Ms. Anderson." Sister

Margaret paced in front of my desk.

"I'm sorry Sister." I wiped the tears from my face.

"It's nothing to cry over darling, I won't call your mother today if it makes you feel better."

I smiled weakly at her. I wasn't sure if anything could make me feel better. Even though I had only known Juan for one night, I felt strangely attached to him. Like there was much more to us that we just didn't know about.

"Are you okay?" asked my friend Erika. I felt bad that I hadn't told her about Juan but how do you tell someone that you might be in love with a dream guy, literally.

"Yeah, I'm fine." I lied. Our hallway was unusually loud. I walked up to a group of girls who were all giggling.

"What's going on?" Our school never got any excitement.

"Didn't you hear?" Asked Julia. "There's a really hot boy here."

"Oh that explains it." Erika said in realization. We all went to a girl's private school. Bring in an attractive boy and you're asking for trouble.

"You didn't let me finish, he's looking for you Seleana!", said Julia excitedly. All the girls squealed in excitement.

I turned around confused, and there he was.

"Juan!" I ran and wrapped my arms around his neck. He hugged me back.

"But how?"

Juan handed me a worn out leather book.

"Rule 1, the Realm World makes an exception to a relationship in the case of true love."

I wish to express my deepest appreciation to my Pastor, Bishop Leon Stutzman, for writing the foreword. He is the Pastor and founder of Christ Cathedral Church and the author of *Order Out of Chaos* and *Invisible Lines of Supply.* His insightful wisdom and knowledge has greatly influenced my life. He has been a blessing and inspiration to countless thousands of people.

I am grateful to Dr. Shirley Clark Stallworth, John Stoddard, Pastor Robert Lyons, of The Market Place Ministry, Rosemary Dannin, Louise Plant, LeDon Maddox and Veronica Sanchez Hines for sharing their amazing stories. I have fondly nicknamed them the "magnificent seven" because of their courage and faith. Their life experiences will serve as an inspiration to others looking to live robust and accomplished lives.

There were many people who were instrumental with the preparation of this book. Special thanks to Sherry Couch from the Portrait Palace for photographing "Some of the Amazing People I Met Along the Way" beginning on page 201. I would also like to express sincere gratitude to Vincent and Victoria Halfacre for their photographic talents that are sprinkled through out the pages.

Special thank you to my creative and young author, Veronica Halfacre, for sharing her short story "Seleana's Sweet Dream" which begins on page 293. The short story cover is graced by Celeste Gracelle Valadez. Thank you Celeste for your beauty.

Thanks to my niece, Ja'Niyah Norman, for helping me to recreate a memory from my childhood when I caught a butterfly. Your hand looks wonderful on the cover. ➡

I am thankful to Karen Leaphart for editing the book.
You have been a great blessing and you are much appreciated!

I am appreciative of my parents, Bishop Edward and Mary Wilson, who taught me at a young age to have unwavering faith in God. I am grateful for the love of my entire family including three brothers and two sisters: (Mark, David, Stephen, Elizabeth Anne and Karen) in addition to a special cousin, Leonard Bo Wilson. Thank you for allowing me to share my thoughts and dreams.

I am grateful to the late Walter and LaVerne Halfacre.
Stewart was blessed with his father's artistic skills
and his mothers kind and caring heart.
I am thankful to be blessed with their son.

Sincere thanks to my husband, Stewart, for all of his support and for the design and layout of this book. There is no way to repay him for all of his hard work. I pray that God will reward him greatly. Thank God for my daughters, Akiya, Veronica and Victoria, whom I love dearly. I pray that they will always strive for excellence and dream big.

Most of all thanks to the reader for this prodigious opportunity to share my life and dreams with you. My prayer is that you will enjoy your journey in life and remember never to stop dreaming.

I thank God each day for all his many blessings!

# Stephanie W. Halfacre
## Living in the DREAM

Stephanie Wilson Halfacre was born in Dayton Ohio and grew up with two sisters and three brothers. She has an Associate Degree in Business Administration. As an ordained minister and inspirational speaker for over 30 years, she enjoys spreading the word of God through counseling and prayer. Stephanie presently serves as a staff pastor at Christ Cathedral Church in Dayton Ohio. She has been happily married to Stewart for 17 wonderful years. Her love for him is as strong today as it was 17 years ago. Stephanie is also the mother of three beautiful daughters, Akiya (Tia), Veronica and Victoria.

When she is not working her "8 to 5" job, Stephanie is busy building her Mary Kay Cosmetic Consultant Business. The Mary Kay business has afforded Stephanie many opportunities to empower women with low self-esteem, including volunteering her services at the Artemis Center of Dayton (an agency dedicated to helping women suffering from domestic violence). She always considers it an honor to share the hope of God and remind women that there is a way out of any destructive situation. Stephanie lives by the motto, "Yesterday is gone, tomorrow will never come, choose today to make a change and don't look back." ➲

In 2011, Stephanie completed her first book, "DreamQuest, A Journey of Significant Vision". She also launched DQ Spirit Works, a publishing company dedicated to sharing the inspirational "works of God" in people's lives. As CEO of DQ Spirit Works, she wants others to live their dreams and experience the grace of God.

In her leisure time, Stephanie enjoys traveling on cruises to the Caribbean, walking for exercise and spending quality time with her family and friends.

For more information about publishing or to schedule speaking engagements, contact Stephanie via —

phone -
937.235.0970

email -
stephhalf@gmail.com

**PEACE.**

God can make your DREAMS a reality!

**May all your dreams come true!**
*May God Bless You, Steph*

ALL PRAISES TO GOD...
HE IS THE MAKER OF DREAMS

MERRY CHRISTMAS
Love & Blessings. The Halfacre Family

**Dream on...** It has been 15 years since the release of my book.
We are grateful to GOD for blessing our growing family.
See video update via https://youtu.be/oN0CYgtEySo
or scan the QR code with a smart phone

**DREAM**QUEST . A Journey of Significant Vision